THE CRAZY WORLD OF

?WHAT IF...

SPACE

AIRPLANES

THE EARTH

THE HUMAN BODY

GIRAFFES

SHARKS

© Aladdin Books Ltd 1996
Designed and produced by
Aladdin Books Ltd
28 Percy Street
London W1P 0LD

This Edition Exclusive to

(949) 587 9207

Editor: Jon Richards
Design: David West Children's
Book Design
Designers: Rob Shone, Flick
Killerby, Edward Simkins
Illustrators: Peter Wilks – Simon
Girling and Associates
Tony Kenyon and John Lobban –
B. L. Kearley Ltd

Printed in China

ISBN 1-55280-164-0

A CIP catalogue record for
this book is available from the
Library of Congress

IMPORTED BY/IMPORTE PAR
DS-MAX CANADA
RICHMOND HILL, ONTARIO
L4B 1H7

ENGLAND
WENTWALK LTD.
278A ABBEYDALE ROAD, WEMBLEY
MIDDLESEX, HA0 1NT

MALAYSIA
PRO ENTERPRISE SDN BHD
LOT 605, SS13/1K, OFF JLN.
KEWAJIPAN, 47500 SUBANG JAYA
SELANGOR D.E., MALAYSIA

DS-MAX
IRVINE, CA 92618
IMPORTER: #16-1241510
949-587-9207

CONTENTS

SPACE 6

AIRPLANES 34

THE EARTH 62

THE HUMAN BODY 88

GIRAFFES 118

SHARKS 144

GLOSSARY 172

INDEX 175

THE CRAZY WORLD OF

?WHAT IF...

SPACE

AIRPLANES

THE EARTH

THE HUMAN BODY

GIRAFFES

SHARKS

Steve Parker

Copper Beech Books

Brookfield, Connecticut

WHAT IF THERE WERE NO INTRODUCTION?

Well, you wouldn't be reading this! The Crazy World of *What If...?* looks at things from a very unusual angle, making them exciting and interesting, as well as being packed with facts and fun.

The universe is unimaginably vast. Have you ever wondered what else might be out there? Well, read chapter one, *What If Space...?* which describes how the Universe works, what's above our heads, and how stars are born, live, and die. It looks at how we have taken our first steps into space and who might be out there, waiting for us.

Do you like flying? If so, you'll know what an amazing experience it is. Peek into, around, and behind various aircraft in chapter two, *What If Airplanes...?* to see how and why they work. You can find out about the pioneers of flying, how the jet engine makes its screaming whine, why flying boats were once popular, and what happens if planes fly upside down. How do pilots fly in the dark? Which planes travel to the edge of space?

Take a look at our Earth, from its very beginnings to what it is like today, in chapter three, *What If The Earth...?* Read about how the Earth swirls through space, what's going on deep beneath our feet, and how the wind, waves, and weather work. Learn about how we are damaging our home planet and what we can do to help save the Earth.

In chapter four, *What If The Human Body...?* you will read how your body is made inside, and how it works. It shows the body's inner parts, how they fit together, and what they do. It explains how you breathe, move, eat, and grow. Learn how to stay healthy and keep your body clean.

Today over 4,000 species of mammal live with each other and even feed off each other, in every part of the world. The state of this planet has been shaped by mammals more than any other group of animal, and by one mammal species in particular – humans. Chapter five, *What If Giraffes...?* describes the world of mammals, and explains how they breathe, grow, live together, and survive.

Nearly seven tenths of the Earth is covered by water. This wet world has provided a superb environment for one of the most diverse groups of animals – fish. Some fish have developed a bizarre collection of features, from the poisonous spines of the lionfish to the electric organs of the catfish. Who knows what other fascinating shapes are to be discovered in the depths of the world's oceans? Learn about these discoveries and many more in chapter six, *What If Sharks...?*

This Crazy World of *What If...* looks at all these amazing aspects of our world in a way that's easy to read and remember, by asking what might happen if... things were different!

THE CRAZY WORLD OF

SPACE

CONTENTS

8   What if the telescope hadn't been invented?

10 What if space weren't space?

12 What if a space probe tried to land on Saturn?

14 What if we had many moons?

16 What if comets didn't return?

18 What if the Sun went out?

20 What if there were no stars at night?

22 What if the universe started to shrink?

24 What if there were no spacecraft?

26 What if rockets hadn't been invented?

28 What if the spacesuit hadn't been invented?

30 What if we could travel at the speed of light?

32 What if there were Martians?

WHAT IF THE TELESCOPE HADN'T BEEN INVENTED?

We would know very little about outer space, where stars, planets, moons, comets, and other objects hurtle at incredible speeds across unimaginably vast distances. Our knowledge about space was given a great boost by the Italian astronomer Galileo Galilei. In 1609 he turned a new-fangled telescope heavenward and saw the Moon and planets magnified. It was a new era in astronomy, the study of space, stars, and other heavenly objects. People have been star-gazing with telescopes ever since.

Geocentric or heliocentric?

Long ago, people believed in a geocentric system where the Sun and all the planets orbited the Earth. However, astronomers, such as Galileo, found that their observations did not match this theory. They proposed a heliocentric system, where the Earth orbits the Sun. Today, we know this system was correct.

Galileo's improved telescope made objects look much larger. He saw that our Moon has mountains and craters, and that Jupiter has its own moons.

How could we see galaxies?

Even without a telescope, you can see a galaxy. The faint streak across the night sky is called the Milky Way, which is made up of millions of stars. It's actually our own galaxy. Telescopes reveal millions of other galaxies, or clusters of stars, in space.

Size isn't everything

The universe is everything, including the Earth, the planets, the Sun, the stars, and space. Without telescopes, we couldn't see very far across the universe. With telescopes, we can detect incredibly distant objects. Scientists use these instruments to measure not only how large the universe is, but also how long it has been around.

Why did an eclipse cause fear and terror?

Until people realized what happens during a solar eclipse (see page 15), these events caused panic and alarm. Many thought that angry gods were destroying the world, or that a massive dragon was trying to eat the Sun!

What if telescopes worked without light?

They do. Light rays are just one tiny part of a whole range of rays called the electromagnetic spectrum. Stars send out light and other rays, such as X rays and gamma rays, into the spectrum. Radio telescopes with large dishes or long aerial wires and satellites detect the rays, to give us yet more information about space.

Earth
Mercury
Venus
Sun
Mars
Jupiter
Asteroid belt

WHAT IF SPACE WEREN'T SPACE?

The space between stars, planets, and other objects is not a complete vacuum (totally empty). There's a lot of emptiness, but there are rays and waves such as heat, light, radio waves, and X rays. There's also the odd molecule of hydrogen and other substances, sometimes forming huge clouds, called nebulae, that may be billions of miles across. There are also tiny particles, bits of dust, and pieces of rock called micrometeors, whizzing around. Near the Earth there's debris such as old rockets and satellites, space-station refuse, lost tools, and other waste. They all make spacewalks rather risky!

Where is space crowded?

In the asteroid belt, between Mars and Jupiter. Asteroids, also called *minor planets*, are big lumps of rock. They vary from about 312 miles (500 km) across to less than 333 feet (100 m). Millions of them make traveling through the asteroid belt very tricky!

What's a shooting star?

A famous movie actor with a gun? No, a shooting star is a lump of rock, called a meteor, that rushes through space and travels close to Earth. As it enters our atmosphere and pushes through the air, the friction, or rubbing, against the air molecules, makes it hot. The meteor glows redhot and burns up, creating a flash, or trail of light, known as a shooting star (falling star). A large meteor might not burn up completely, and can crash onto the Earth's surface as a meteorite.

What if there were air in space?

There would be no need for spacesuits since we could breathe. There would be no need for rockets either, since jet or propeller engines can work in the air. Birds could fly through it, too.

How high up is outer space?

Just above the Earth's atmosphere! As you go higher above the Earth's surface, the air gets thinner and thinner. Eventually there is almost nothing left, and you are in outer space. But there's no obvious dividing line. Normal air has all but disappeared by 62 miles (100 km). The top layer of the atmosphere, the exosphere, begins at about 250 miles (400 km) above the ground. Yet the first "space" satellite, Sputnik 1, orbited the Earth as low as 143 miles (230 km).

Could we land on Venus?

Venus is similar in size to the Earth. But its atmosphere has clouds of corrosive sulfuric acid, and the surface temperature is 869°F (465°C). Not the place for a vacation!

Which planet is not named after a god?

All of the planets are named after Roman or Greek gods, except for Earth. It is named after the Old English word, "eorthe," meaning land or soil.

WHAT IF A SPACE PROBE TRIED TO LAND ON SATURN?

It would be very difficult, because there is hardly any "land" to land on! Saturn is the second largest planet, 75,335 miles (120,536 km) across, made up of mainly hydrogen and helium. A space probe would pass the planet's beautiful rings and disappear into the immense gas clouds of the atmosphere. As the probe fell deeper, the pressure would increase, and before long crush the probe. Further down, the pressure is so great that the gases are squeezed into liquid. The planet's core is a small, rocky lump.

The planet of fire and ice

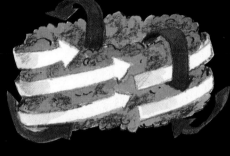

Mercury, the planet closest to the Sun, is only 3,048 miles (4,878 km) in diameter. Its atmosphere has been blasted away by powerful solar winds. This rocky ball has daytime temperatures ranging from over 806°F (430°C) – hot enough to melt lead – to a bone-chilling -292°F (-180°C)!

Stormy weather

Jupiter has a storm three times the size of Earth, about 25,000 miles (40,000 km) across. It's called the Great Red Spot, and drifts around the planet's lower half. A gigantic vortex sucks up corrosive phosphorus and sulfur, in a huge swirling spiral. At the top of this spiral, the chemicals spill out, forming the huge spot, before falling back into the planet's atmosphere.

Are there canals on Mars?

Not really. But there are channels or canyons. In 1877 Italian astronomer Giovanni Schiaparelli described lines crisscrossing the surface of the "Red Planet." He called them canali which means "channels."

What are planetary rings made of?

Saturn has the biggest and best rings – six main ones, made up of hundreds of ringlets. They are 175,000 miles (280,000 km) in diameter – more than twice the planet's width. They are made from blocks of rocks, ranging from a few inches to about 16 feet (5 m), swirling around the planet, and covered with glistening ice. Jupiter, Neptune, and Uranus also have fine rings.

Which planet is farthest from the Sun?

Pluto. No, Neptune. No – both! On average, Pluto is the outermost planet. This small, cold world is only 1,438 miles (2,300 km) across, with a temperature of -364°F (-220°C). Its orbit is squashed, so for some of the time, it's closer to the Sun than its neighbor Neptune. In fact, Pluto is within Neptune's orbit until 1999.

WHAT IF WE HAD MANY MOONS?

If the Earth had a lot of moons, night creatures might get confused. Moths use the Moon to find their way around – which would they choose if there were more than one? Owls, bats, and other night creatures might not wake up, as reflected light from the many Moons would keep the night sky bright. The Earth would also be more like the other planets. Most planets have lots of moons going around them. We have only one, which we call the Moon. At 2,160 miles (3,476 km) in diameter, it's much larger than most moons of other planets. With all these new moons we'd have to invent new names for them.

Is there a man in the moon?

No, but there were men on the Moon – the Apollo astronauts between 1969-1972. The patterns that we see on the Moon's surface, which resemble a crooked face, are made of giant mountains and massive craters. The craters, which can be as large as 625 miles (1,000 km) across, were made when asteroids and meteorites crashed into the Moon's surface.

The birth of a moon

Some scientists believe the Moon was probably formed at the same time as the Earth, from rocks whirling in space. Others think it was made when a planet crashed into the Earth, throwing up masses of debris, which clumped together to form the Moon. The moons of other planets may have been asteroids captured by the planets' gravity.

Which planet has the most moons?

At the moment Saturn has the most, with 18 moons as well as its colorful rings. This is followed by Jupiter with 16, and then Uranus which has 15. However, as telescopes get bigger and better, more moons may be discovered, so these numbers may change.

What happens if the Moon goes in front of the Sun?

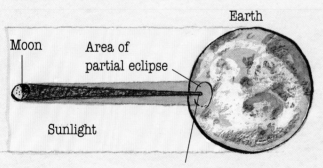

Moon   Area of partial eclipse   Earth

Sunlight

Area of total eclipse

It blocks out the Sun and casts a shadow on Earth, and we get a solar eclipse. But this does not happen all over the world. The total eclipse, with all the Sun hidden, is only in a small area. Around this is the area of partial eclipse, where the Sun appears to be only partly covered.

What's on the far side of the Moon?

The Moon goes around the Earth once every 27 days 8 hours. It also takes 27 days 8 hours to spin on its own axis. So the Moon always shows the same side to us. The far side of the Moon was first seen by the spacecraft Luna 3 in 1959, which sent back photographs of a lifeless moon, with no partying aliens!

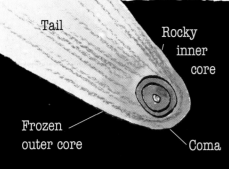

Tail

Rocky inner core

Frozen outer core

Coma

Inside a comet

A typical comet has a small center, or core, a few miles across. It's made from pieces of grit, dust, and crystals of frozen gases such as methane, ammonia, carbon dioxide, and water (ice).

WHAT IF COMETS DIDN'T RETURN?

Ancient civilizations thought a comet was a god breathing into the heavens or sending a fireball to destroy the Earth. At regular intervals they would streak across the night sky, creating fear and panic in all who saw them. Comets are really just lumps of ice and rock that boil and fizz as they near the Sun, sending out a huge tail of dust and vapor. In the 1700s it was noticed that some comets kept returning, orbiting the Sun in a stretched-out circle, called a *parabola*. Some just disappear into deep space.

Crash, bang, smash

If a comet hit a planet, there would be a massive explosion. This was seen when the comet Shoemaker-Levy 9 collided with Jupiter in 1994. A series of explosions punched huge holes in the atmosphere, stirring up gases from Jupiter's interior.

How do we know comets will return?

The British astronomer Edmond Halley noticed that the paths of comets observed in 1531 and 1607, and the one he saw in 1682, were all the same – was it the same comet returning each time? He predicted it would return in 1758. It did, and has since been called Halley's comet. From his theories, astronomers were able to plot comets' long orbits around the Sun.

How do we know what's inside a comet?

From observing its orbit and how fast it travels, by studying the light and other waves it gives out, and with space probes and telescopes. In 1986, five space probes passed near Halley's comet, on its regular visit. Europe's Giotto got within 375 miles (600 km) of the core, which is only 10 miles (16 km) long and 5 miles (8 km) wide, and sent back many photographs.

What if a comet didn't have a tail?

For much of its lifetime, it doesn't. As a comet travels close to the Sun and warms, its icy crust boils, throwing out gases that make a glowing outer layer, called the *coma*. The solar wind blows dust and other particles from the coma to form a tail that reflects the Sun's glow, and points away from the Sun. Then the comet heads into space, and the tail disappears.

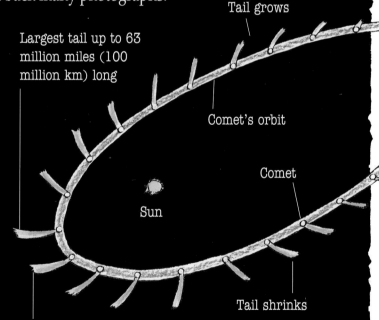

Tail grows

Largest tail up to 63 million miles (100 million km) long

Comet's orbit

Comet

Sun

Tail shrinks

Tail points away from Sun

How long do comets last?

Some fall to pieces after a few hundred years, while others may last millions of years. It depends partly on how often the comet travels near the Sun. Halley's comet has been seen every 75-76 years for over 2,000 years!

WHAT IF THE SUN WENT OUT?

Who turned off the lights? Why is it suddenly so cold? If the Sun no longer bathed our world in light and warmth, we might last a short time with fires, electric light, and oil or gas heat. But plants could not grow in the dark, and animals would perish from the cold. Soon all life would cease, and our planet would be dark and frozen. In fact this will happen, but not for billions of years. Our Sun is a fairly typical star, and stars do not last forever. They form, grow old, and either fade away or explode in a supernova, a massive explosion.

From the cradle to the grave

Throughout the universe there are massive clouds of gas, called *nebulae.* In some of these, the dust and particles clump together, and over millions of years, these clumps will form stars. Other nebulae are the wispy remains of a *supernova,* a star that has exploded.

What is a red giant?

An enormous human with red clothes? No, it is a star that has been growing and shining for billions of years, and is nearing the end of its life. As it ages, the star swells and its light turns red. Our Sun will do this in millions of years. It will expand to the size of a Red Giant, scorching our planet, before it explodes. Then all that will be left is a tiny white dwarf star that will slowly fade over millions of years.

How can we see a black hole?

When a really big star explodes, its core collapses and leaves behind a remnant whose gravity is so strong that nothing can escape its pull. This remnant is called a black hole. Because light cannot escape, it is impossible to actually see a black hole. However, its presence can be detected by the effect it has on objects around, such as gases, and waves, including light rays and X rays.

Great balls of fire

A typical star is made mainly of hydrogen gas. Huge forces squeeze together its atoms to form helium. This process is called *nuclear fusion*. As the atoms fuse they release energy, which radiates from the core, through the radiation zone. The energy is then carried to the surface by circular convection currents. Finally at the photosphere, the energy is radiated into space as light and other types of rays and waves.

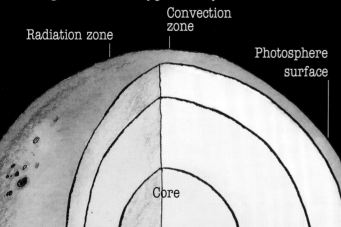

Radiation zone

Convection zone

Photosphere surface

Core

Silent explosion

Sound waves can't pass through the vacuum of space, so we can't hear a star explode. But we can see it, as a glow that appears in the night sky, which then fades. It leaves behind a cloud, called a *nebula*.

Dizzy galaxies

A galaxy is a group of billions of stars. Our own galaxy is called a spiral because it spins like a pinwheel. Other types of galaxies are ellipticals (oval) or irregulars (no shape). There are many other spiral galaxies like our own.

How did ancient civilizations view the universe?

Many ancient cultures were fascinated by the stars. According to some theories, the ancient Egyptians tried to construct a replica of the heavens on Earth, with the Nile representing the Milky Way, and the three great pyramids as Orion's belt.

WHAT IF THERE WERE NO STARS AT NIGHT?

Sometimes there aren't, if it's cloudy. Well, the stars are still there, but we can't see them. Without stars, the ancient Greeks and others wouldn't have spent hours gazing at them. They could see the outlines of people, animals, and objects in the star patterns. The constellations, which include Orion (the Hunter), Scorpio (the Scorpion), and Centaur (half man, half horse), are based on figures from Greek myths. Navigators couldn't have found their way across the seas and oceans without using the stars.

Zoo in the sky

The stars in the night sky are divided into patterns and groups, known as constellations (see above). These were named after people from legends, objects, and even animals. The northern hemisphere has two bears: The Great Bear (Ursa major), and The Little Bear (Ursa minor). Find some star charts and try to look for them tonight. The night sky also has a bird of paradise (Apus), an eagle (Aquila), a ram (Aries), a toucan (Tucana), a wolf (Lupus), two dogs (Canis major and Canis minor), a whale (Cetus), and a snake (Serpens).

What if the stars moved?

They do. Stars in our spiral galaxy are spinning around. Our Sun takes over 200 million years to orbit the center of the galaxy. As the stars move, star patterns and constellations gradually change. In thousands of years, constellations will be different, and today's star charts will be out-of-date.

What if planets shone, like stars?

It would probably never get dark! Planets shine, but only because they reflect the light from the Sun. However, they are not massive enough to start the process of nuclear fusion which makes stars shine (see page 19).

WHAT IF THE UNIVERSE STARTED TO SHRINK?

Echoes in space

Radio telescopes picking up microwaves detect a background "hiss" in space. It shows the temperature of the universe is slightly warmer in some parts than others. These "ripples" are echoes of the Big Bang.

Most experts believe that the universe began as a tiny speck containing all matter, which blew up billions of years ago in a massive explosion, called the Big Bang. It's been getting bigger ever since, as galaxies fly away from one another. This may go on forever, or the universe might reach a certain size, and then maintain a steady state, or it could begin to shrink. All the planets, stars, galaxies, and other matter might squeeze back together to form a tiny speck as the opposite of the Big Bang – the Big Crunch.

What was the Big Bang?

It was the beginning of the universe: the time when all matter began to explode and expand, from a small core full of incredible heat, light, and energy. Was there anything before the Big Bang, like a supreme being? No one knows. There may have been no "before." Space, matter, energy, and even time may have started with the Big Bang.

Strings and clusters

Our galaxy is only one of millions found throughout the universe. Together with a few others, such as the Andromeda galaxy, it forms the Local Group, a collection or cluster of galaxies that circle around space together. The Local Group is, in turn, part of a group of galaxy clusters known as a supercluster. These superclusters are linked by massive strings of galaxies that may be up to 300 million light-years long.

How far can we look across our universe?

As telescopes become more powerful, and orbit in space on satellites, they can pick up the faint light and other waves from more distant stars and galaxies. The farthest object currently visible is Quasar (QUASi-stellAR object) 4C41.17. This object is so far away that light reaching us now left the galaxy when the universe was one-fifth its current age.

Happy birthday to you...

The general agreement is that the universe was "born" in the Big Bang about 14 billion years ago. Some believe that it is closer to 17 billion or as low as 10 billion years old. Scientists are still arguing about its exact age. You would need a very big cake for all the birthday candles!

WHAT IF THERE WERE NO SPACECRAFT?

How would astronauts get back to Earth?

An astronaut could survive in a spacesuit for a short time. But coming back into Earth's atmosphere creates lots of heat, as an object pushes through the ever-thickening air molecules. A heat shield might help a rear-first re-entry!

Space exploration would be much less exciting without spacecraft that carry people. It began with the Space Race in the 1950s and 1960s. The United States and the former Soviet Union raced to launch the first satellite, the first spaceman and woman, and the first Moon visit. The satellite *Sputnik 1*, launched in 1957, was the first man-made object in space, and the Russian Yuri Gagarin was the first man in space. But the United States was first to land on the Moon in 1969 with the spacecraft *Apollo 11* carrying Neil Armstrong and Edwin "Buzz" Aldrin. Without spacecraft, none of these achievements would have happened.

What would Yuri Gagarin have done?

Yuri was the very first person in space. On April 12, 1961, he orbited Earth once in his ball-shaped spacecraft, *Vostok 1*. Without this spacecraft, he would never have become world famous. But he could have carried on as a successful test pilot for the Russian Air Force.

What if there were no satellites?

We would have no satellite TV or satellite weather pictures, and mobile phones would not work very well. Ships, planes, and overland explorers could not use their satellite navigation gadgets. Without satellites, countries would have to find new ways to spy on each other. They could go back to the high-flying spyplanes used just after World War II, or use high-flying balloons carrying surveillance equipment.

How much money would we save?

Space programs run throughout the world by different countries, like the Apollo Moon missions, have cost billions of dollars. Manned space flights are the most expensive type of missions. It has been estimated that NASA has spent over $80 billion on its manned space flights up to 1994, with nearly $45 billion spent on the space shuttle program alone! Even a single spacesuit worn outside the space shuttle costs $3.4 million!

Nonstick earthlings

Our everyday lives have been affected by the enormous technological leaps made during the age of space exploration. These "leaps" include nonstick coatings, used for lubrication in spacecraft. Also, the microtechnology needed in satellites has led to smaller and faster computers, some found in household appliances.

WELCOME EARTHLINGS!

WHAT IF ROCKETS HADN'T BEEN INVENTED?

We would still be wondering about the empty space above us, instead of launching astronauts into space and sending probes on space missions. A rocket can fly fast enough to get into space. To do this, it must reach the speed called escape velocity, 17,700 mph (28,500 km/h), to escape from the pull of Earth's gravity. A rocket engine can work in airless space, unlike jets and other engines, as explained below. The other way to get into space might be a gigantic gun that fires spacecraft and satellites into space. However, any astronaut would be crushed by the g-forces of acceleration!

Dawn of the rocket age

The first rockets used a type of gunpowder and flew in warfare in China, in A.D. 1232. The first modern rocket to use the liquid fuel that today's rockets use was launched by American scientist Robert Goddard in 1926.

Why can't jets fly in space?

Like a jet engine, a rocket burns fuel in a type of continuous explosion. Hot gases blast out of the back, and thrust the engine forward. Space has no air, which is needed for the burning that takes place inside the jet engine. A rocket must carry its own supply of oxygen.

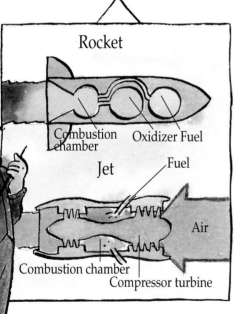

Rocket

Combustion chamber   Oxidizer Fuel

Jet   Fuel

Air

Combustion chamber
Compressor turbine

Rockets and jets
Rockets carry their own oxidizer substance. Jets, however, need oxygen from the air to burn their fuel.

Up, up, and away in my beautiful balloon

Special weather balloons go higher than 31 miles (50 km). They carry radiosondes that measure temperature, air pressure, and humidity, and send back the results by radio. The balloon is quite small and floppy when it takes off, but it gradually expands as it rises, as the air pressure decreases. However, no weather balloon could carry a heavy satellite high enough, or give it the required speed to put it in orbit.

Would we have fabulous firework displays?

Perhaps, but we would have to power the rockets by other types of engines, maybe a mini jet engine. Firework rockets use solid fuel such as gunpowder or other fuel-oxidizer mixtures to launch into the air. Many space rockets use liquid fuel, and have the propellant and oxidizer in liquid form.

Multi-staged rockets

A staged rocket may have two, three, or more rockets, placed on top of each other in decreasing size. The biggest one launches the entire rocket, then stops firing and falls away. The rocket's weight is now less and so is the effect of the Earth's gravity, so the second-stage rocket is much smaller, and so on with the remaining stages. Extra rockets, called boosters, may assist the main rocket engine at launch and then fall away, as in the space shuttle.

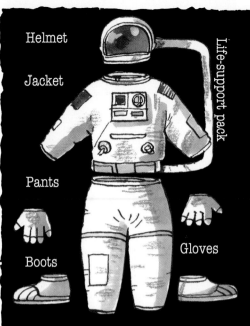

Helmet

Jacket

Pants

Boots

Gloves

Life-support pack

Sections of a spacesuit
The suit has various parts, and it takes a long time to put on. All the joints must be airtight, to maintain proper air pressure and temperature.

WHAT IF THE SPACESUIT HADN'T BEEN INVENTED?

Astronauts are safe in space, if they stay inside their spacecraft. Outside, there is no air to breathe, and it is incredibly cold (or hot). There are lots of dangerous rays and radiations, and micrometeors travel as fast as tiny bullets. The space suit is shiny to reflect rays of radiation. It contains its own *life-support systems* that control the air and temperature. It also has special layers to protect against impact from debris. In space, any other type of suit, like a deep-sea diver's suit, would be no good at all!

How could we repair satellites?

If a satellite malfunctions, astronauts can maneuver their spacecraft near it, then float over in a spacesuit with a jet-pack, to make repairs. If spacesuits didn't exist we might have to invent a robot repairman!

Would Alexei Leonov be so famous?

This Russian astronaut became famous on March 18, 1965. He was first to use a spacesuit to leave his space-craft for a space "walk," floating weightlessly, miles above the Earth.

Could people have landed on the Moon?

Yes, but they wouldn't have been able to walk around. The bootprints of the Apollo astronauts will be in the dust for thousands of years.

Leaky spacesuits

The suit contains a mixture of gases for breathing. It's under pressure, to simulate the Earth's atmosphere. If it squirts away through a leak, the astronaut will be in great danger!

What if spacesuits weren't cooled?

Or warmed, either? In Earth's orbit, the astronaut orbits the planet in about 90 minutes. He would get boiling hot while in the glare of the Sun. As he circled around to the night side, he'd freeze to death! The spacesuit keeps his body temperature within a more comfortable range.

NEAREST STAR
23,700,000,000,000 MILES

WHAT IF WE COULD TRAVEL AT THE SPEED OF LIGHT?

Almost everything in the universe varies from place to place, such as temperature, pressure, gravity, and the size and mass of objects. However, the speed of light is always the same – 186,282 miles per second (299,792 kilometers per second). As you approach the speed of light, strange things happen, according to Albert Einstein's theory of relativity.

What is a light-year?

Is it 365 sunny days? No, it is not a measure of time, but of distance. It's the distance that light travels in one year. Since light travels very fast, a light-year is extremely far – about 5.88 trillion miles (9.46 trillion km) Even so, space is so vast that a light-year is a tiny distance.

Time slows down, and objects get smaller and heavier. Modern science says that no physical matter could travel faster than light, or even at the speed of light. However, radio waves and X rays travel as fast as light, since they are part of the same electromagnetic spectrum.

Space, the final frontier...

In science fiction stories, such as *Star Trek*, characters are always traveling from solar system to solar system in search of adventure. However, even if we could travel at the speed of light, it would still take over four years to reach Proxima Centauri, our nearest star after the Sun. Even then, we would have to find a planet to land on.

NCC-1701

Could we reach the nearest galaxy?

Not unless science came up with some amazing new theories about travel and going faster than the speed of light. The closest galaxy to our own is the Large Magellanic Cloud (LMC), only 17,000 light-years from home! Other nearby galaxies are the Small Magellanic Cloud (SMC), M31 Andromeda, M32, and M33 Triangulum Spiral. Together they form part of the Local Group of galaxies, in our part of the universe. If we tried to go to another galaxy in a spacecraft like the shuttle, it would take millions of years.

How long would it take to get to a planet?

Mars is probably the best example. It's quite close – it's the nearest planet and also has hard ground to land on, as the *Pathfinder* has shown. With current spacecraft technology, the latest journey took 7 months. Mars *Pathfinder* landed on the planet's surface in July 1997. It carried a tiny rover, called *Sojourner*.

Can we live in space?

Yes, although the collision between a supply vessel and the solar panels on *Mir* space station have highlighted the dangers of living and working in space. Such crewed space stations play an important role in the space program. Ideas for the future include giant wheel-shaped stations with their own gravity, like towns in space.

31

WHAT IF THERE WERE MARTIANS?

Are UFOs real?

Unidentified Flying Objects certainly do exist. People, including jet-plane pilots, see things in the sky they cannot identify. But are they alien spacecraft? They could be test planes, meteors, or even the planet Venus!

The space probes, *Vikings 1* and 2, landed on Mars in 1976. They found a reddish, dusty, rock-strewn landscape. But their cameras, sensors, and experiments detected no proper sign of life. In August 1993, as the space probe *Mars Observer* approached its destination, its radio failed, and all went silent. Was it sabotaged by shy, secretive Martians? Probably not. The Mars *Pathfinder* that landed in July 1997, has not reported any sign of life so far. Scientists estimate that among 10 billion galaxies, there are trillions of stars, and probably some that have planets like Earth – maybe these have some kind of life.

Are we trying to send messages to aliens?

Yes, we send bursts of radio messages into space. Also, space probes carry messages in case they are found by aliens. Space probes such as Pioneers 10 and 11 have plaques with drawings of humans, and a star map showing where we are.

Are aliens trying to get in touch with us?

Perhaps, but messages in bottles won't work! Only light, radio, and similar waves travel through space at great speed. Aliens might send messages as coded patterns of waves. Radio telescopes used for the National Aeronautics and Space Administration's (NASA) Search for ExtraTerrestrial Intelligence project (SETI) have failed to detect such waves.

What if they landed?

There's a plan for dealing with aliens, but it's top secret. Anyway, aliens advanced enough for space travel would be much smarter than we are. So it might not matter what we did. We just hope they are friendly!

Evidence of alien landings

A few strange cave drawings, paintings, sculptures, and rock patterns from ancient times, might suggest that aliens visited Earth long ago. Some people say that over the years, aliens have helped us. But there's no real proof, and that's what scientists require.

THE CRAZY WORLD OF

AIRPLANES

CONTENTS

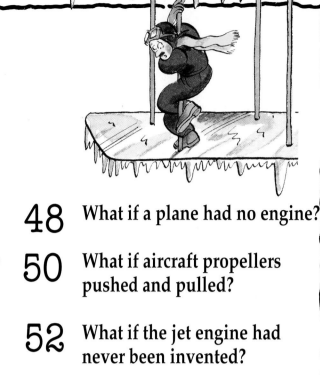

36 What if aircraft didn't have wings?

38 What if animals didn't have wings?

40 What if planes didn't have tails?

42 What if planes could land on water?

44 What if the Wright brothers had stuck to cycling?

46 What if a helicopter had no rear propeller?

48 What if a plane had no engine?

50 What if aircraft propellers pushed and pulled?

52 What if the jet engine had never been invented?

54 What if there were no pilot?

56 What if the pilot got lost?

58 What if there were no airports?

60 What if there were no planes?

WHAT IF AIRCRAFT DIDN'T HAVE WINGS?

Most of them would speed along the runway... and crash at the end, without taking off. Wings make a plane rise into the air, by providing lift. The wing shape also tells you how fast a plane goes. Slower planes, especially gliders, have very long, thin wings that stick out sideways. These wings have a very narrow chord (the distance from the front of the wing – leading edge – to the rear of the wing – trailing edge). This is the same design as the wings of gliding birds, like the albatross. Faster planes have swept-back wings, usually with a bigger chord, like fast hunting birds such as hawks.

An uplifting experience

Some aircraft don't get their lift from wings. It comes from a jet engine or propeller facing straight down, which pushes the aircraft into the air. A strange test craft from the 1950s, called the "Flying Bedstead," did this. So does the Harrier Jump Jet, which can take off straight up, and hover in mid-air. Hovercraft use lifting fans, like propellers facing downward, to create a cushion of air.

What if a plane flew upside down?

First, how does a wing work? Seen end-on, a wing has a special shape, known as the airfoil section. It is more curved on top than below. As the plane flies, air going over the wing has farther to travel than air beneath, and this extra distance means that the air over the top moves faster. This produces low pressure above the wing, so the wing is pushed upward – a force known as *lift* – which raises the plane. If a plane flew upside down, the wing would not give any lift. To overcome this, the plane tilts its nose up at a steep angle. Air hitting the wing pushes it up, keeping the plane in the air.

Air moves faster

Lift

Wing

Air moves slower

Can planes fly in space?

A few can, like the X-15 rocket planes of the 1960s and the space shuttles of today. First, they need engine power to blast up there. The X-15 was carried up on a converted B-52 bomber, while today the shuttle uses massive rocket boosters. Once in space, there's no air (or anything else), so wings can't work by providing lift. The power for all maneuvers in space comes from small rocket thrusters.

How do spy planes fly so high?

Spy planes, such as the U-2 and the Blackbird, need to fly high, at 100,000 ft (30,000 m) or higher, so they are beyond detection by enemy planes or radar. However, as air is very thin at such heights, they need very special wing designs, with an extra-curved top surface, to give the greatest possible lift. With the arrival of spy satellites, the use of spy planes declined, until recently. A new generation of pilotless, remote-control spy planes, such as DarkStar, has arrived.

WHAT IF ANIMALS DIDN'T HAVE WINGS?

They couldn't fly, either. Only three groups of animals can fly with complete control. These are insects, birds, and bats. Many other "flying" creatures, such as flying squirrels, are really only gliders, just able to swoop down to the ground. The true fliers beat their wings up and down, to give both lift and forward thrust. Their bodies have many special features. They are lightweight, yet have strong muscles to move their wings. If humans had wings, our chest and shoulder muscles would need to be huge to flap them, and our legs would be tiny to save weight!

Flying insects

In an insect, like a bee, the middle part of the body, or thorax, contains two sets of muscles. The wings are fixed to the outer case of the thorax. As the muscles contract they pull the wings up and down.

Going batty!

Bats fly by flapping their arms, which have become long, large wings during millions of years of evolution. A bat's finger bones are extremely long. They support the wing membrane, which is incredibly thin, yet stretchy and strong. The fingers can make the wing twist to change direction, and fold it away after use as an upside-down sleeping bag!

Membrane

Fingers

How do birds fly?

They go flap-flap-flap! As in bats, the bird's arms have evolved into wings. Very strong muscles in the chest pull the wings down. This pushes air down, and pushes the bird up. The wings and feathers are angled so that some air is pushed backward too, giving the bird forward movement. Smaller muscles pull the wings up. During this upstroke the feathers twist so that air can pass through them, otherwise the bird would just push itself down again!

Thin walls

Cross-struts

What if a bird wanted to save weight?

Natural evolution has already produced lots of weight-saving features. These include thin-walled bones with air spaces for lightness and cross-struts for strength. Feathers also weigh hardly anything, yet they give a bird a streamlined body, a warm coat, and colors for camouflage.

A load of hot air

Birds can stay up for hours by using rising currents of warm air, called thermals. The bird circles around these to rise up, before gliding to another thermal. Glider pilots also use thermals to stay aloft.

Thermal

Human-powered flight

Human legs are strong enough to get the body airborne, with a little help from machinery. The Gossamer Albatross crossed the English Channel between France and England in 1979, using only a human cyclist to keep it in the air.

WHAT IF PLANES DIDN'T HAVE TAILS?

They would be impossible to steer or control! The tail has important parts called stabilizers and control surfaces. The upright stabilizer, or fin, stops the plane from swinging side to side. Attached to the back of the fin is the rudder, for steering left to right. The small, rear stabilizers, or tailplane stop the plane from wobbling up and down. Hinged to their rear are the elevators, for climbing or diving.

Aileron

Controls roll, which is the plane leaning or tilting to the side, for turning, or even spinning right over in a corkscrew-like path.

Rudder
Controls yaw, which is the plane turning left or right.

Are there planes without tails?

Yes, a few. Stealth planes are designed to be invisible on radar, so they lack an upright stabilizer (fin) because this shows up well on radar.

What if engines were at the back?

Some are! However, you would have to move the tailplane and fin somewhere else. The fin's task might be done by vertilizers (vertical stabilizers) at the ends of the wings. The tailplane's job could be done by small foreplane wings at the front, called *canards*.

Elevator
Controls the plane pointing up or down, for climbing higher or diving lower.

How many wings does a plane need?

In the early days, when wing design was just beginning, and engines were not very powerful, many planes, called biplanes, had two sets of wings. The Phillips Multiplane of 1907 had 21 small, thin wings! But it crashed into pieces.

What if planes were like paper darts?

One almost is. Concorde has long, triangular wings along the sides of the fuselage (body), called *delta wings*. These give good lift and stability at high speeds, since Concorde cruises at more than Mach 2 (twice the speed of sound) – 1,320 mph (2,125 km/h).

Swinging wings

Some planes have swing-wings. They are called "variable geometry" combat jets, and they take off and land on a very short runway, such as the deck of an aircraft carrier. The wings swing sideways for take off, slow flight and landing, and then swing back for superfast speed.

WHAT IF PLANES COULD LAND ON WATER?

Many can. In an emergency, the pilot can "ditch" the plane onto water. It's very risky and the plane usually sinks – but at least the crew and passengers have a chance of survival. Seaplanes are different. They are designed to take off and land on water. Instead of wheels, they have long, streamlined floats that slip smoothly over the surface. The flying boat is a type of seaplane with a boat-shaped fuselage (body) that rests in the water. Flying boats were popular when air travel began in the 1930s. Few big cities had airports with long runways, but many were near water. Today, seaplanes are useful in places that have many islands and few landing strips.

Can seaplanes land on land?

Some can. They have wheels that stick out slightly below the floats, so they can touch down on water or land. They are called *amphibious aircraft*. One problem is that floats are quite large, so they make the plane fly slower and use more fuel, compared to wheels which can be retracted.

Skimming above the waves

One of the latest developments for seaplanes is the *ground effect* plane. Developed by Russia, the ground effect plane traps air underneath its wings to create a cushion, on which the plane skims over the waves. A hovercraft uses the same principle.

Which boat has wings?

The hydrofoil is a boat that has ski-like wings on stilts under its hull. As it picks up speed, the wings provide lift in the water (like a plane's wings in the air). This makes the hull rise out of the water. The hydrofoil can then travel at great speed because less of the boat is in contact with the water, skimming across the surface.

How big are seaplanes?

The flying boat Hughes H4 Hercules, nicknamed the Spruce Goose, has the longest wingspan of any airplane, at 327 ft (98 m) – as big as a soccer field. A Boeing 747 Jumbo Jet's wings are 200 ft (60 m) long. The H4 was built in 1947 and flew only once, just 3,000 ft (1,000 m).

Can aircraft land on ships?

Yes. Helicopters can land on a small platform which can be fitted to any reasonably sized ship. Navy ships called aircraft carriers have a long, wide, flat deck for takeoffs and landings by special carrier-borne planes. These shipboard jet fighters include the Sea Harrier Jump Jet, the F-14 Tomcat, and the F-18 Hornet.

WHAT IF THE WRIGHT BROTHERS HAD STUCK TO CYCLING?

Yes, it's true. Wilbur and Orville Wright were really bicycle mechanics! In the late 19th century, the new craze was the "safety cycle." In their hometown of Dayton, Ohio, the Wright brothers set up a business manufacturing and selling bicycles. In 1903, they attached an engine to a glider and produced the *Flyer*. Orville piloted the *Flyer* on the world's first airplane flight December 17, 1903 at Kitty Hawk, North Carolina.

What if Louis Blériot had taken off late?

He might not have been first to fly the English Channel, on July 25, 1909. He had to fly between dawn and dusk, so the aviator took off from Calais at 4:40 a.m. After traveling 23 miles (37 km), he landed in Dover, England.

On the rocks!

Between June 14 and 15, 1919, British airmen John Alcock and Arthur Brown made the first non-stop flight across the Atlantic Ocean. They flew from Newfoundland, Canada, to Ireland, in a converted Vickers Vimy. In a snowstorm, a fuel gauge became iced over. So Brown climbed out to knock the ice away. A build up of ice could have caused the plane to crash!

How did Charles Lindbergh stay awake?

He had to – he was first to fly solo non-stop across the Atlantic, from New York to Paris, on May 20 to 21, 1927. The trip, in his Ryan Monoplane *Spirit of St. Louis*, was 3,631 miles (5,810 km) and took 33 hours 29 minutes. A former airmail pilot, Lindbergh dozed off several times. He woke as the plane went out of control, diving and spinning toward the waves. But he quickly became alert when he reached Ireland's rocky coast, and flew on to a huge crowd in France.

Do planes get faster and faster?

They certainly do! Since the first powered flight by the Wright brothers, people have tried to fly faster and faster. The Wright *Flyer* managed about 31 mph (50 km/h) in its short flight at Kitty Hawk. By the 1930s, planes, such as the GB Sportster (above) were zooming through the sky at 296 mph (477 km/h). Since then, the advent of the jet and rocket age has pushed airplanes faster. The fastest airspeed was achieved in a Lockheed SR-71A "Blackbird," flying at 2,193 mph (3,530 km/h) in 1976.

WHAT IF A HELICOPTER HAD NO REAR PROPELLER?

The main "propeller" on top of a helicopter is the main rotor, and the small propeller at the rear is the tail rotor. Without a tail rotor, as the main rotor spun around one way, the helicopter would spin the other! This is due to a basic law of science – Newton's third law of motion, which says that every action has an equal and opposite reaction. So the pilot and passengers would get very dizzy and the helicopter would be impossible to control!

How are the rotor blades controlled?

By a complicated device in the middle of the rotors, called the *rotor head*. It has a double ring, called the swashplate. The lower ring is moved up and down and tilted by the pilot's control levers and pedals, and the upper one spins with the rotors. By a complicated system of hinges, levers, and bearings, the swashplate makes the rotors change their height and pitch (slope or angle), to give more lift for climbing, or less lift for descending.

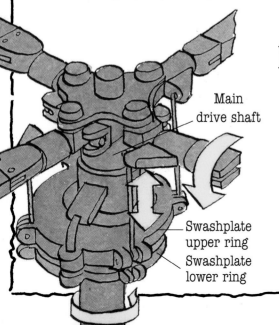

Main drive shaft

Swashplate upper ring

Swashplate lower ring

What if a helicopter had two main rotors?

Their blades might crash into each other! If the rotors were at slightly different heights, and linked by gears, their blades could always move between each other. This happens on twin-rotor helicopters like the CH-47 Chinook. The rotors go in opposite directions, so there's no need for a tail rotor.

What if a rotor had no engine?

Can a plane fly like a helicopter?

The Bell-Boeing V-22 Osprey can. Its engines and propellers can tilt, so that the Osprey can take off or land vertically and even hover, like a helicopter. The engine then slowly tilts forward so that the Osprey can fly normally.

An autogyro has a normal engine and propeller, and a large helicopter-like rotor that is unpowered. The forward movement makes the rotor swirl around and provide lift, so this craft doesn't need wings.

Is it difficult to fly a helicopter?

For most people, yes. The helicopter is an unstable design, and without the pilot's constant attention, it would spin out of control. Foot pedals control the tail rotor. The cyclic pitch control lever in front tilts the rotors to fly forward, backward, or sideways. The collective pitch control lever at the side alters the rotors to climb or descend. Its engine throttle twist-grip changes engine speed. That's five controls at once!

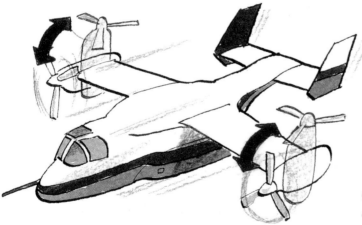

Cyclic pitch control lever

Collective pitch control lever

Rudder pedals

WHAT IF A PLANE HAD NO ENGINE?

Most planes can glide down in an emergency, like when the engine is falling out. But a plane that's designed to have no engine is a glider, or perhaps a hang glider. These unpowered aircraft sail and soar silently through the air. They always glide downward against the air around them, but they do so very gradually, because of their light weight and excellent aerodynamic shapes. The best gliders travel over 196 ft (60 m) yet descend only 3ft (1 m). The key to gliding is to find air that's moving upward faster than your glider is going downward, such as a thermal (see page 39). A cockpit instrument called the compensated variometer shows how fast the air outside is moving up or down, no matter what the vertical speed or maneuvers of the glider itself. Once in this rising air, the glider will circle, and gain height.

How do gliders take off?

In the past, gliders have been launched off cliffs, and catapulted by bungee cords. Some were even towed behind cars. One method used today is the fast-running winch that winds in the tow-rope attached to the glider. Most popular is aero-towing behind a small plane.

Do some pilots hang around all day?

In a hang glider, the pilot hangs below a large V-shaped wing made of flexible material stretched over a metal-tube frame. The pilot steers by shifting his or her body weight to make the aircraft move up, down, or sideways. The world-record distance for a real glider is 913 miles (1,460 km), and for a hang glider, 305 miles (488 km).

Which glider fits in a backpack?

The modern parachute has several sections called *cells* and works partly like a glider. It can be controlled and steered by pulling on cords. Using one of these parachutes, and helped by thermals, a parachutist can stay in the air for 40 minutes.

What if your parachute didn't open?

This hardly ever happens. Parachutes are thoroughly checked and packed very carefully into their bags, so that they open properly every time. However, there is a reserve parachute for use in emergencies, because it is smaller.

Getting heavy!

Big military gliders can carry troops and several tons of equipment, such as large guns and even jeeps. A jumbo-sized glider could even carry jumbo-sized cargo such as elephants! The world's biggest glider is the space shuttle, which comes down to land at 219 mph (350 km/h).

WHAT IF AIRCRAFT PROPELLERS PUSHED AND PULLED?

They do, depending on which way they spin. So it's important to make the engine work only one way, or the plane might shoot backward! A propeller (prop) at the front pulls the plane, while the one at the back pushes it. Both work in the same way, as shown below.

Can propellers work at the back?

Back propellers are known as *pusherprops*. They spin and work in the same way as *pullerprops* (front propellers). They're used in modern microlights and slow-flying survey aircraft. With a pusherprop, the pilot has a good view and does not get wind and noise from the blades. But aerial control is better with pullerprops.

How do propellers work?

Air pushed backward

Forward thrust

First, each blade has an airfoil section, like a mini-wing. It creates low air pressure in front and higher air pressure behind. This pulls the plane forward.

Secondly, a propeller's long blades are angled. As they rotate, they push air backward and pull themselves forward.

How many blades can a prop have?

The number depends on features such as the size and power of the engine turning it, the design of the whole plane, and how fast you want to go. Many planes have two-bladed props. Multi-bladed props are heavier and need more powerful engines.

What if a propeller was attached to a jet?

It is, sort of. A turbofan is a jet engine with a huge, multi-bladed fan turbine at the front. This blows air at high pressure into the engine, as in a normal jet. It also blows air around the engine, like a prop (see page 52).

Fan turbine

Combustion chamber

How big can propellers be?

Well, their blades must be shorter than the plane's landing gear and wheels, or they would smash into the ground! Also, longer blades mean the tips go faster. If the tip speed reaches the speed of sound, about 763 mph (1,220 km/h), the prop may vibrate and shatter. Larger props must rotate slowly.

Why didn't war pilots shoot off their propellers?

In World War I (1914–1918), fighter planes had just been invented. At first, pilots shot with hand-held pistols or rifles. A machine gun in front of the pilot, where he could see to take aim, would be a good idea – but the bullets might hit the propeller! So in 1915, the designers of the German Fokker fighters invented a levers-and-gears device called the *interrupter*. It made sure the bullets fired between the blades as they whizzed around.

WHAT IF THE JET ENGINE HAD NEVER BEEN INVENTED?

Air travel and air battle would be much slower. The fastest jetliners, and the fastest military fighter and bomber aircraft, are all powered by jet engines. Only jets can move the average airliner along at 563 to 593 mph (900 to 950 km/h), which is nearly the speed of sound. An airliner with the other main type of propulsion, piston (internal combustion) engines turning propellers, could never keep up – no matter how many engines it had! And only jets can accelerate some fighters to more than 1,625 mph (2,600 km/h), like the McDonnell Douglas F-15 Eagle and the Russian MiG-25 Foxbat.

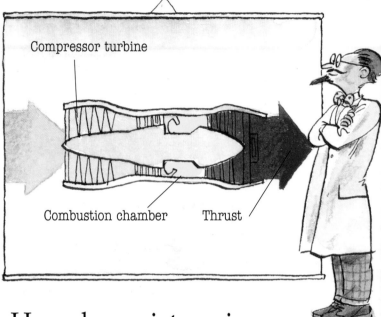

Compressor turbine

Combustion chamber   Thrust

How does a jet engine work?

It uses spinning angled blades called turbines, which work like powerful, high-speed fans. The jet engine sucks in air at the front, squeezes and squashes it with the compressor turbines, sprays fuel into it, and burns it in the combustion chamber as a continuous roaring explosion. The hot gases blast out of the back, and thrust the jet engine forward. As the gases leave, they spin the exhaust turbines, which are linked to, and drive, the compressor turbines. Other jets include the ramjet and turbofan (see page 51).

What if the whole engine spun around?

On some planes, it does! It's called a rotary engine and works basically like a car engine, with pistons going up and down inside cylinders. But a rotary engine has its cylinders in a circle, and they spin around and around.

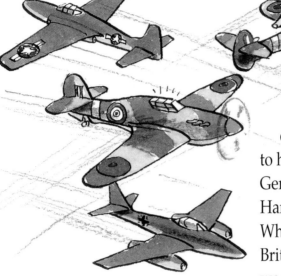

Which were the first propless planes?

The first jet engines were revved up by English engineer Frank Whittle in 1937, but they were firmly fixed to his test bench. The first jet-powered airplane to fly was the German Heinkel He 178 in 1939, with an engine designed by Hans Pabst von Ohain. It was followed by the British Gloster Whittle, in 1941. The first jet aircraft to enter service was the British Gloster Meteor fighter, but the first to get into a fight was the Messerschmitt Me 262, in September 1944.

Silent night

Modern designs of turbofans are much quieter than the earlier turbojets. But many other things affect aircraft noise, such as the height of the plane. If an aircraft can take off very quickly and climb rapidly – Short Take-Off and Landing (STOL) – it soon seems quieter to people on the ground. Many city airports have rules governing noise limits and allow only STOL aircraft.

Could aircraft break the sound barrier?

Without jets, probably not. The fastest propeller-driven aircraft ever flown is the Russian TU-95/142, nicknamed the "Bear." It has been recorded flying at 575 mph (925 km/h) – that's four fifths the speed of sound. Almost, but not quite.

WHAT IF THERE WERE NO PILOT?

Sometimes there isn't. At least, not a human pilot actually operating the controls. Many modern planes have an automatic pilot. It's not a robot sitting in the pilot's seat, but a set of controls incorporated into the main controls. The real pilot sets the plane's speed, height and direction, then switches to automatic, for a break. Of course, if something happens, alarms activate, and the real pilot takes the controls. In very modern planes, the computer-based auto-pilot can even take off and land the aircraft.

How do pilots "fly by wire?"

Computer screens are wired up to show speed, direction, engine conditions, and other information. Small levers and switches activate the flaps, rudder, and other control surfaces. This happens by sending electrical signals along wires to motors. This system is all controlled by the avionics system.

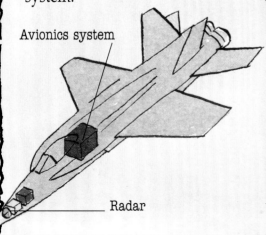

Avionics system

Radar

What is a "black box?"

It's not usually black or box-shaped. It may be bright orange and cylindrical. But it's the usual name for an aircraft's flight data recorder. This device continually records the plane's speed, height, direction, and other information from the instruments, as well as radio signals and voice communications. It is specially made to be fireproof, shockproof, and waterproof. In the event of emergency or disaster, it can be recovered, and its recordings give valuable information about what happened.

Tires, skis, skids, and floats

Airplanes can be equipped with a variety of landing gear, depending on their size and the conditions. Jet liners require wheels to withstand the pressure. Seaplanes need floats to keep them above water. Gliders and early rocket planes use skids, while planes that have to land on snow and ice use skis!

Do you have to be strong to fly a plane?

Not really. Some controls are simple electrical switches and knobs. Others are levers, like the control column and rudder pedals, but they are well-balanced with counterweights and cables, so they aren't too heavy to move. But to fly a plane well, you do have to be alert and physically fit, with good coordination and quick reactions.

When can you see two sets of controls and instruments?

In the "head-up display." There are not really two sets. Part of the main display is reflected or projected upward onto the front windshield or canopy, or into the pilot's special helmet visor. The pilot can look ahead and see outside and the controls at the same time.

WHAT IF THE PILOT GOT LOST?

Can pilots see in the dark?

They can "see" using radar (RAdio Detection And Ranging). This works like a bat's hearing. It blips out radio signals, and detects the echoes that bounce off other planes or features, and then displays them on a screen. Radar was first used in World War II (1939 – 1945). To keep it secret, there was a rumor that the pilots ate lots of carrots to see in the dark!

A lost pilot could mean big trouble. He or she couldn't stop and ask someone the way. An airplane has a limited amount of fuel, and, sooner or later, it must land. What if the pilot is lost flying over mountains at this time, or thick woodland? What if it becomes foggy, or dark, and the pilot can't find the runway? This is why all pilots must learn about navigation: knowing where you are and where you're going. It can be done by many methods, such as using a compass and radar signals from ground beacons. The pilot can also talk to an air-traffic controller, and use modern satellite navigation, as well as looking out of the window!

Highways in the sky

The skies near busy airports get crowded, so there are flight corridors for planes going in certain directions. Each plane must know where to fly, and the speed and height it must travel – its flight path. The whole system is organized by air-traffic controllers, who speak to all planes by radio and by positional satellites. They make sure that there are no near misses (or should that be near hits?)

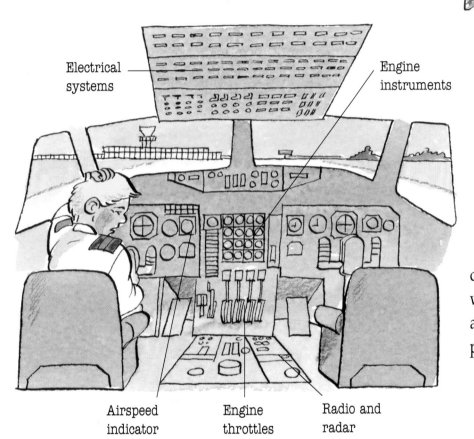

Electrical systems

Engine instruments

Airspeed indicator

Engine throttles

Radio and radar

How do pilots tell time?

In a modern jetliner, the time is one of several pieces of important information displayed by the instruments on the flight deck. These include air speed, altitude (height), a compass to show direction, and a radio to stay in touch with the ground control. The displays are on computer screens. A small plane simply has an ordinary clock!

How do pilots talk to people?

Not by shouting loudly! They talk over the plane's radio, mainly to air-traffic controllers in their control towers on the ground, and perhaps to the pilots of other planes, or meteorologists at weather stations. They might also chat to people from the airline about flight times or special passengers, or to the plane manufacturers if the aircraft is behaving strangely. The radio plays a vital role in keeping the pilot informed about what is happening outside the plane.

WHAT IF THERE WERE NO AIRPORTS?

Are there airports in cities?

Not in the very center. A plane taking off couldn't stop at red lights! But there are small airports very close to the city centers. They are used mainly by helicopters, small business jets, and STOL commuter planes (see page 53). Big airliners need very long runways and make too much noise, so their airports are usually several miles away from city centers. There are usually urban highways and public transportation to the city airports.

Landing a huge jetliner in a field would be impossible. It might hit a molehill or sink in the mud. Even if it landed, the passengers would not be pleased to find themselves in the middle of nowhere! Many modern planes need a straight, flat, hard-surfaced runway at least 9,842 ft (3,000 m) long, for safe takeoff and landing. In fact, most airports have two or more runways, facing different directions. This is because it's best for planes to take off or land into the wind. The air blowing at the plane and over the wings creates increased lift for the same speed relative to the ground. This gives quicker lift off and better control on touchdown.

Why can't you stack planes on top of each other?

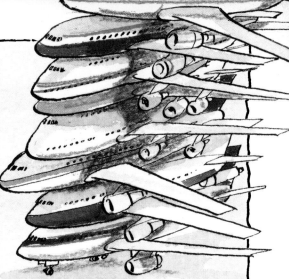

You can, if you are an air-traffic controller (see page 56). As planes wait to land at a busy airport, they fly in wide circles at certain heights, each several hundred feet above the next. When the runway is clear, the lowest one takes its final approach path and comes in to land. The others move down the stack level, one by one, from the lowest upward.

What if there were no air-traffic control?

At a busy international airport there is a takeoff or landing every 30 seconds. The air-traffic controllers speak by radio to the pilots, telling them which approach paths to follow, where to stack, and which runway to use for takeoff and landing. Otherwise, CRASH! BANG! SMASH! CRUNCH!

Slam on the brakes

Many planes have brakes on their wheels to stop. Jets may have panels that fold out to deflect their exhaust gases forward. Other planes may use parachutes, or if they are to land on an aircraft carrier, a trailing hook that catches on wires on the deck.

How do planes land in the dark?

The pilot does not use a flashlight or eat lots of carrots (see page 56). There are landing lights and radio beacons near the airport showing the direction and distance of the runway, and patterns of colored runway lights illuminating the landing area. Many planes have an Instrument Landing System (ILS). It detects radio signals sent from the airport to show if the pilot is landing safely.

WHAT IF THERE WERE NO PLANES?

Life would certainly be different. Airplanes play many vital roles throughout the world, carrying people and cargo to faraway places in only a fraction of the time it takes other forms of transportation. The sky might be full of balloons, slowly weaving about the sky. Instead of crossing the Atlantic in a couple of hours, it would take several days on an ocean liner, or stuck in a small basket under a balloon.

Can saucers fly?

They certainly can. Have you ever thrown a Frisbee and wondered why it can fly? That's because the shape of a Frisbee is similar to a plane's wing. It has an airfoil section which creates a higher pressure below its body than above as it passes through the air, producing lift. It achieves all this without the help of wings. Many planes can achieve the same effect by having their fuselage (body) shaped with an airfoil cross-section. They are known as *lifting bodies* and can fly with only very small wings.

Would other forms of transportation be the same?

Without the luxury of aircraft to fly us around the world at incredible speeds, other forms of transportation would have to change to adapt, in order to carry the increased number of passengers. We would have to build very long trains and enormous city buses that would travel along highways. Without planes, the ground would quickly become crowded with cars and buses carrying people around.

Could we travel as quickly?

The fastest train in the world is the Train à Grande Vitesse (TGV) of France. It zooms across the countryside at an amazing 320.2 mph (515.3 km/h). This is easily as fast as many small aircraft, but is nothing compared to the superfast jet planes that regularly fly over our heads. Planes can also fly over oceans, whereas trains and passengers have to go on ferry boats.

A bridge over troubled waters

With over two thirds of the world covered in water we would need some way of quickly traveling between islands and continents. This could be achieved by building extremely long tunnels and bridges, stretching over the horizon. Some have been made already, such as the Channel Tunnel linking England and France, and the Seven Mile Bridge linking the Florida Keys.

THE

EARTH

CONTENTS

64 What if the Earth stood still?

66 What if there were no magnetic field?

68 What if the Earth were twice as big?

70 What if the Earth were smaller?

72 What if the continents didn't move?

74 What if there were a lot more volcanoes?

76 What if there were no wind?

78 What if the water ran out?

80 What if we had storms every day?

82 What if there were no soil?

84 What if fossil fuels ran out?

86 What if the ozone hole gets worse?

WHAT IF THE EARTH STOOD STILL?

Direction of Earth's spin

Axis of spin

If it were daytime, the first thing you might notice was that the Sun stopped moving across the sky. You'd wait for evening – but it would never come. It'd be daylight forever! The Earth spins around like a gigantic top on an imaginary line called its axis, that goes through the North and South Poles. It makes one complete turn every 24 hours, giving us the cycle of day and night. As your area of the surface turns, the Sun appears to move across the sky in daytime, and the stars and Moon move across at nighttime.

A still Earth would heat up unbearably on the daytime side.

Daytime on the side facing the Sun

A hard day's night!

If we had endless daytime, the Sun would shine without a break and you might get sunburned. You would also have to go to sleep in bright daylight. People on the other side of the Earth would be in constant cold and darkness. They would become pale and sick.

On the shady side, it would be dark, cold, and soon freeze over.

No more seasons in the Sun?

Besides spinning like a top, the Earth also goes around the Sun in a long, curved path called its *orbit*. One orbit takes one year. The Earth's spinning axis is tilted, so some parts of its surface are closer to the Sun during certain times in the orbit. On these closer parts it is warmer – and summer. If the Earth stopped orbiting and stood still, the seasons would cease, too. It would be endless summer in some areas, and everlasting winter in others!

Sun

Summer in south

Spring in north

Fall in north

Summer in north and winter in south

Winter in north

Nighttime on the side away from the Sun

What would happen to clocks and calendars?

Clocks would keep ticking, and we might continue to use them to tell time. But this would be less useful. We could no longer say things like "It gets dark at 8 o'clock." The calendar would be less useful, too. Without seasons, every month would have the same weather and you would soon get very bored!

How might animals react?

They'd get very confused! Their internal "body clocks" need the pattern of night and day to stay accurate. With no day or night, they wouldn't know when to eat or sleep. With no seasons, they wouldn't know if they should begin a winter's sleep (hibernation) or set off for a long fall or spring journey (migration).

APRIL

OCTOBER

JULY

DECEN

The best place to live

A still Earth would have a very narrow strip on each side, one in constant dawn, and the other in continuous dusk. These areas would not get too bright and hot or too dark and cold. They'd be the best places to live.

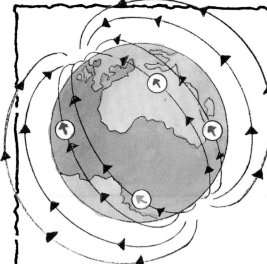

The Earth's magnetism is probably made by the swirling movements of molten iron-rich rocks deep inside the planet. Compass needles align with the invisible lines of magnetic force.

WHAT IF THERE WERE NO MAGNETIC FIELD?

The compass needle would point anywhere! A compass needle is a very long, thin, lightweight magnet labeled North and South. The Earth is like a giant magnet with North and South Poles. When the needle swings freely, it always points toward the Earth's magnetic North Pole. A basic law of magnetism says "unlike poles attract." The compass needle's South Pole is attracted to the Earth's magnetic North Pole. If the compass needle pointed anywhere, many people who rely on compasses – from pilots to mountaineers – would soon get lost!

The world upside down

With no magnetic field a compass wouldn't be any help when you tried to follow a map. Maps are usually drawn with North at the top and South at the bottom. If the compass pointed anywhere, there would be no North or South. So you could make a map showing the countryside any way up! Note that a compass points to the magnetic North Pole, not the geographic North Pole around which the Earth spins. Because of the way the magnetism varies, these two poles are many miles apart. The same happens with the magnetic and geographic South Poles.

The Great Age of Exploration was made possible by the compass. Explorers used it to chart their courses. It was hard to get directions from people who spoke a very different language. Compasses made directions easier!

The natural world of maps and compasses

Some animals make long journeys called migrations, from summer feeding and breeding places, to winter resting places. Whales, bats, reindeer, birds such as geese and terns, and butterflies do this. Many seem to find their way by a combination of the layout of the land and sea, the position of the Sun, Moon, and stars – and the Earth's magnetism. These animals might have "body compasses" inside them, that show which way they are heading in relation to the Earth's magnetic field.

A very magnetic prospect!

When oldtime prospectors were searching for gold or gems, they worked mainly by trial and error. Today, modern science uses devices which can measure the tiny variations in the Earth's magnetism. The magnetic force of the Earth can be changed by rocks rich in iron or iron compounds. It can also be altered by pools of oil and gas, or deposits of salt and other minerals, which are found deep under the surface.

How could ships and planes find their way?

The compass is still important for long journeys by boat, plane, and off-road vehicles. But in the last few years, the 21 main satellites of the Global Positioning System (GPS) have been placed around the Earth. They send out radio signals and a receiver-decoder unit detects them. It shows your position to an accuracy of 328 feet (100 m), anywhere in the world!

WHAT IF THE EARTH WERE TWICE AS BIG?

With all distances doubled, people would spend more time traveling. The equator would be much longer and the North and South Poles further apart. Objects attract each other with a natural pull called gravitational force. If the Earth were twice as big, its gravity would be greater. Things pulled harder by this increased gravity would weigh more – including you!

Could plants still grow?

Probably, but they would be affected by the stronger downward pull. They'd be shorter, stockier and stronger, so that they could hold themselves up against the greater gravity. A tree house in the tallest tree might be down near the ground! All plants would have to grow shorter and stronger. So would animals and people. You'd develop stronger muscles to move your extra weight, and so you'd weigh even more than before!

Extra gravity would make things fall faster, and pull the ink out of your pen in a flood – an inkfall!

How might a bigger Earth move?

As the Earth whizzes through space on its orbit around the Sun, it has a certain amount of energy. To obey the laws of physics, a heavier Earth would have to keep its amount of energy. So it might move further from the Sun, and orbit the Sun at a greater distance. This would have many effects, such as …

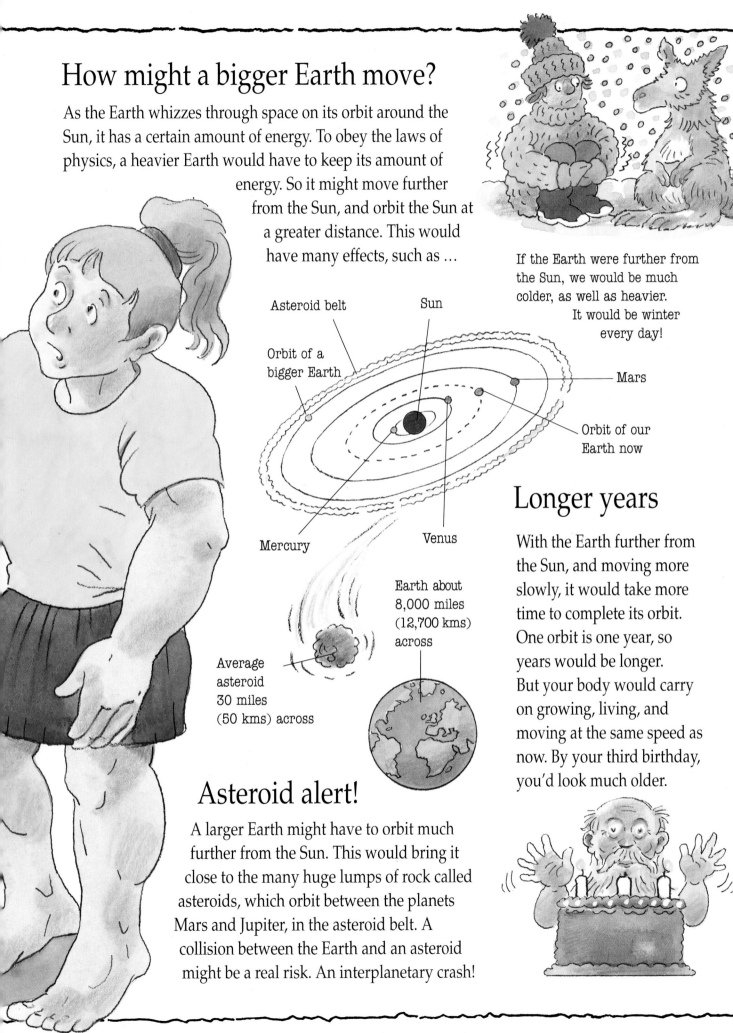

If the Earth were further from the Sun, we would be much colder, as well as heavier. It would be winter every day!

Asteroid belt

Sun

Orbit of a bigger Earth

Mars

Orbit of our Earth now

Mercury

Venus

Earth about 8,000 miles (12,700 kms) across

Average asteroid 30 miles (50 kms) across

Longer years

With the Earth further from the Sun, and moving more slowly, it would take more time to complete its orbit. One orbit is one year, so years would be longer. But your body would carry on growing, living, and moving at the same speed as now. By your third birthday, you'd look much older.

Asteroid alert!

A larger Earth might have to orbit much further from the Sun. This would bring it close to the many huge lumps of rock called asteroids, which orbit between the planets Mars and Jupiter, in the asteroid belt. A collision between the Earth and an asteroid might be a real risk. An interplanetary crash!

WHAT IF THE EARTH WERE SMALLER?

You could get to school sooner, and go everywhere else quicker, too. All distances would be shorter. People would be nearer each other, so we might feel more overcrowded. Also, a smaller Earth would have less gravity, so you would weigh less, and you could jump higher and further than you can now. It would be like being on the Moon, which is one-quarter of the size of the Earth. However, less gravity would hold less atmosphere near the ground, so the air would be thinner. This might cause lots of changes …

The perfect body?

The human body would be much slimmer, since it would not need strong muscles to hold it up and move it around against the weaker gravity. If the air were thinner, though, we'd need much bigger lungs to breathe in enough of it, in order to get the oxygen we need. So people and animals might have huge barrel-shaped chests.

Would the apple have fallen on Newton's head?

Yes. But it would have fallen more slowly, because of the weaker gravitational force. It could have taken many minutes, and Newton might have fallen asleep! If the apple had fallen gently onto his head, it might not have startled him into thinking about the laws of gravity and motion, back in the 1660s (if the story is true – some say it's a myth.) In any case, without his great work, science might now be centuries behind.

1hr
2hrs
3hrs
4hrs

Keeping hold of the Moon

Without the strong gravitational pull of the Earth which keeps the Moon in its orbit, it might simply float away into space. We would see it getting smaller each night, until it disappeared into space. Then we would have no Moon.

Over the speed limit!

A moving object pushes through the billions of floating molecules (like nitrogen and oxygen) which make up air. The pushing slows the object – this is called *air resistance*. If the air were thinner, there would be fewer molecules, and less air resistance. Objects could go faster, and streamlining would be less important.

Keeping your feet on the ground

With no gravity at all, everything would be weightless, like it is in space. You could float along with no effort, and lift a car or even a huge boat, or train. However, you might float up and away, into the sky, and never be able to get back down again!

WHAT IF THE CONTINENTS DIDN'T MOVE?

The land under your feet may seem solid and still. But each main landmass, or continent, is drifting very slowly across the face of the Earth, by less than 2 inches (5 cm) each year. The Earth's outer "skin," or crust, is made up of 12 giant, curved plates, like a vast, ball-shaped puzzle. They are called *lithospheric* (curved-rock) *plates*. As the plates rub against each other, their edges crack or get pushed deeper. Some plates enlarge, while others shrink. This has been going on since the Earth began, 4.5 billion years ago.

We would see some strange animal meetings!

The plates under the ocean are thinner. Molten rock from deep below becomes solid, adds to the plate, pushing it sideways.

An oceanic plate pushes into a continental plate. The oceanic plate is forced down and an ocean trench forms.

Continent

Ocean

Magma (molten rock)

Rock steady

Without continental drift, there could be no metamorphic rocks, like marble. These form when other rocks are squeezed incredibly hard in the roots of new mountains. Igneous rocks, like granite, form when melted rock, such as the lava from volcanoes, cools and solidifies. Sedimentary rocks, such as chalk, form when tiny particles settle in a lake or sea, and get pressed and cemented together.

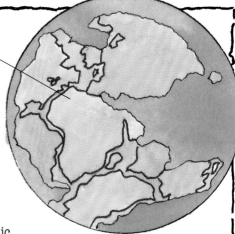

Pangaea

Metamorphic rock

Igneous rock

Sedimentary rock

Mapping out the world

About 250 million years ago all the continents were joined into one vast land mass, the super-continent of Pangaea. The continuous ocean around it was the Tethys Sea. If continental drift had stopped, the map would still look like this. A journey from North America to Europe, or South America to Africa, could be by car!

The layers of rock in the continental plate are crumpled by movements. This creates huge folds – mountains.

Highs and lows!

The world would be much flatter and less exciting without continental drift. The deepest part of the oceans, the Marianas Trench in the Pacific, and the highest mountain, Mount Everest in the Himalayas, wouldn't exist.

Fold mountains

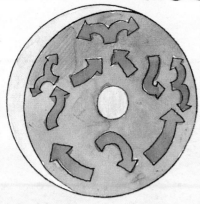

The molten rocks of the Earth's middle layer, or mantle, flow around slowly like thick jelly or soft plastic.

WHAT IF THERE WERE A LOT MORE VOLCANOES?

You'd have to be careful where you went because a volcano could erupt anywhere, at anytime! Below the Earth's hard outer surface (crust), the rocks are so hot that they are melted. Sometimes the pressure builds up so much that these melted rocks burst through a crack in the crust. This is a volcanic eruption, and the red-hot rock that comes out is known as lava.

From volcano to paradise island

Volcanoes that erupt under the sea build up layers of hardened lava, and poke above the water as islands. Coral reefs develop around their shores. Earth movements make the island sink. The coral continues to grow, leaving a ring-shaped reef called an atoll.

Undersea volcano erupts.

Hardened lava builds up and coral forms.

Island sinks, more coral forms atoll.

Full steam ahead for "Old Faithful?"

"Old Faithful" is a famous geyser in Yellowstone National Park. Geysers spurt a fountain of hot water and steam from a hole or crack in the ground. The water has trickled through many tiny crevices deep down into the rocks, and has become heated until it boils and blasts back out along a crack or tube. "Old Faithful" goes off about every hour and squirts water nearly 150 feet (46 meters) high. But slowly, over thousands of years, geysers lose their heat and power, and die with a final puff.

Quake, rattle, and roll!

The world would be a much safer place without earthquakes. Those that occur in populated areas topple buildings, crack roads and railways, and ruin lives. Most earthquakes happen where the giant curved plates, which form the surface of the Earth (see page 72), are rubbing against each other. The plates stick for a time until immense forces build up, then they move with a jolt, sending out shuddering shockwaves.

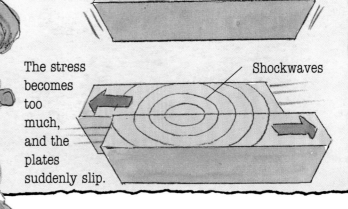

Plates try to move, but the edges stick and forces build up.

Fault line

The stress becomes too much, and the plates suddenly slip.

Shockwaves

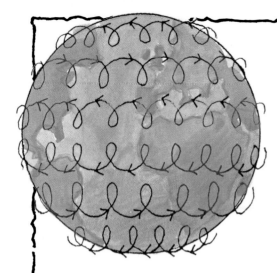

WHAT IF THERE WERE NO WIND?

The world would be extremely boring! There would be no kites, sailboats, windsurfers, or cool breezes on a hot day. The air would stagnate as mist, clouds, and pollution hung around forever. We have wind because the Sun's warmth heats the air, the hot air rises, and cooler air blows in to take its place. No wind? No way!

The Sun's heat is generally stronger around the equator than closer to the poles. Also, the daily spinning of the Earth means that each patch of its surface goes from warm day to cool night. The Earth's orbit around the Sun gives seasonal changes of hot summers and cold winters. All these temperature differences create general wind patterns around the world.

Lower cool air moves sideways to fill the gap. This is wind.

Like hot air from a fire, Sun-warmed air rises.

What would the famous explorers have done?

Not a lot – without wind to push their sailing ships around the world, the Great Age of Exploration and Discovery might never have happened with Christopher Columbus (1492), Ferdinand Magellan (1519), Sir Francis Drake (1577), and James Cook (1768).

The Beaufort Scale measures wind speed by its effects on waves, trees, and buildings. It was invented by Admiral Beaufort in 1805.

1 No wind

3 Leaves move

5 Waves whipped up

8 Difficult to walk

10 Trees fall over

12 Devastation

Weather or not...

The wind affects our weather as it blows cool air to warm places, lowering temperatures. Wind also blows clouds that drop rain. This creates climate patterns, which affect the plants and animals that can live in a certain area.

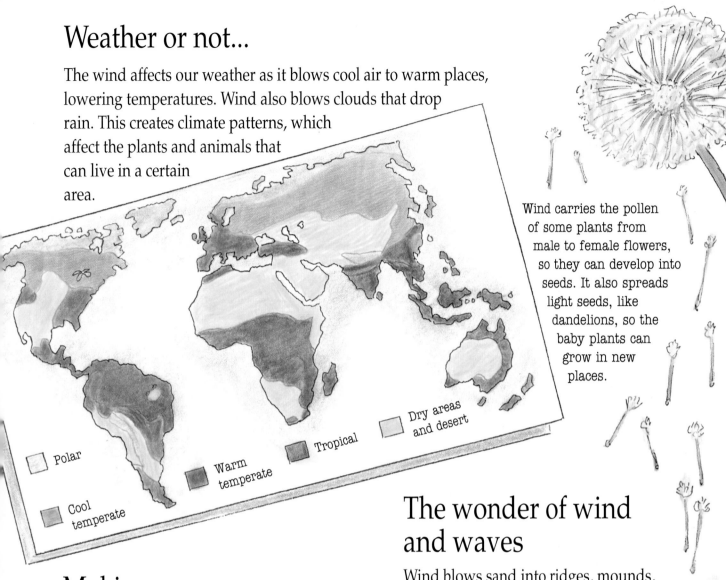

Polar

Cool temperate

Warm temperate

Tropical

Dry areas and desert

Wind carries the pollen of some plants from male to female flowers, so they can develop into seeds. It also spreads light seeds, like dandelions, so the baby plants can grow in new places.

Making waves

With no wind, the seas and oceans would be very calm. The effects of wind blowing over the ocean create huge ripples, called swell. (You can make a miniature version by blowing across your bath water.) As the swell moves into shallow water, the ripples pile up and then roll over with a white, foaming crash. Beaches would be calm and quiet without waves; safe for young children, but boring for surfers!

The wonder of wind and waves

Wind blows sand into ridges, mounds, hills, dunes, and other shapes, which creates an interesting beach landscape. (This happens in sandy deserts as well as on the beach.) Waves move the sand grains around, rub and smooth the grains, wash and clean them, and carry away dirt and garbage. So, a windless, waveless beach would probably be quite flat, featureless, and dirty.

WHAT IF THE WATER RAN OUT?

Gradually, the whole world would dry up. Rivers, lakes, and oceans would disappear, as would clouds and rain. All plants and animals would die, since water is essential for life. Luckily this does not happen, because of the water cycle. The same water keeps going around and around as in the diagram, above left. Very little new water forms, and hardly any old water is destroyed. The same water is naturally recycled.

Rain

Rivers

Seas

Water vapor

Water that flows along rivers into the seas is warmed by the Sun and evaporates into the air as invisible water vapor. It then condenses in a cloud to form droplets and falls back to Earth as bigger drops of rain – which drains into a river... and the cycle starts again. The Sun powers the cycle, by warming water to make it evaporate and rise.

Could the rainforests survive?

Without water they would be first to be affected. A typical rainforest needs at least 100 inches (250 cm) of rain each year – three times more than in Seattle, Washington. Without it, leaves shrivel and the trees die. There would be fewer rain-carrying clouds and more sunshine, increasing the drying effect. Rainforest creatures would be made homeless and suffer from thirst and sunstroke.

Would farmland suffer?

Certainly. Less rain would mean poorer crops, especially those which need lots of moisture, such as rice and potatoes. The lush, grassy pastures grazed by cows and sheep would also dry out. We'd all be affected as food became scarce and expensive. It would take many years to breed new, drought-resistant crops. Camel meat might become very popular!

What would happen to the mountains ?

They would not be covered in snow, ice, glaciers, frost, and rushing streams, so the rocks would erode less quickly. Very old mountains, such as the Appalachians, would still be tall, sharp and jagged, instead of lower, smoother, and rounded.

Water, water everywhere, but...

If the water on land ran out we'd have to turn to the seas for drinking water. We can't drink salty seawater, but we can evaporate water vapor from it, to get rid of the salt, using the heat of the Sun or boilers. The water vapor is condensed to make fresh drinking water (like a miniature water cycle). This is called *desalination*, and is done today in hot, dry places, like the Middle East.

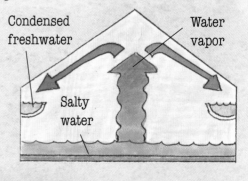

Condensed freshwater

Water vapor

Salty water

WHAT IF WE HAD STORMS EVERY DAY?

If the weather went out of control, we might get storms with wind and rain – every day! In fact this already happens in a few places in the world. A mountain in Hawaii has only fifteen non-rainy days each year. Mawsynram in India has ten times more rain every year than New York City. If the world were this wet, floods would soon cover the land, forming lakes and rivers in low-lying areas. Crocodiles and fish could swim into places that were once deserts!

What's a tornado?

A tornado is a small area of fast-swirling, violent wind, shaped like a tube or funnel. Hanging below a thundercloud (cumulonimbus), they tend to form over land, and are the most powerful winds. The part of the tornado on the ground is often only 165-330 feet (50-100 meters) across, and it moves along at about 10 miles (15 kms) per hour. The fierce winds of a tornado can whirl around at 280 miles (450 kms) per hour. It can suck up and destroy anything in its path.

What's inside a hurricane?

An area that is warmer, calmer, and clearer than its surroundings! It's called the eye, and it can be about 12.5 miles (20 kms) across. Around it, incredible winds swirl counterclockwise at speeds of at least 75 miles (120 kms) per hour, and often even more. There's heavy rainfall, too – over 8 inches (20 cm) in a few hours. That's as much rain as Oregonians see in four months.

Eye

Strongest winds

Air circulates counterclockwise

Most rain

Positive electrical charge

Negative electrical charge

Would there be more lightning?

Probably. In a storm cloud, fast-moving air swirls around, rubbing tiny, floating water droplets together. This rubbing causes a buildup of electrical charge, or static electricity. When there is too much, the electricity "jumps," as a gigantic spark, to another cloud or to the ground. The intense heat of the spark makes the air around it boil and expand faster than the speed of sound. The spark is a lightning bolt, and the expanding air is a thunder clap.

Lightning bolt

Keep away from isolated tall objects!

Would our homes and buildings change?

Ordinary storms, wind, and floods can damage houses. If we had extra storms, we'd have to change our building designs. A house might have an extra-strong roof that could not blow off, and waterproof doors and windows to keep out the water. Or the house could be on tall stilts, so that the water passed harmlessly underneath, and with a roof that could be repaired easily. There are already houses like this in parts of the world prone to hurricanes, storms, floods, and tidal waves.

WHAT IF THERE WERE NO SOIL?

You wouldn't get scolded for getting your clothes muddy or dirty! But there would be hundreds of problems. Earthworms, moles, ants, and millions of other burrowing creatures would be homeless. Plants could not set down their roots in soil, or take in water, nutrients, and minerals for their growth. We'd have no farm crops, and nothing for farm animals to eat. We'd all starve!

A game of two halves!

Many sports, from football to soccer, are played on soil. Rather, on soil covered with well-mown grass. It's fairly soft and doesn't hurt too much if you fall. Without grass and soil, we'd have to play these sports on astroturf.

Soil soaks up rain like a sponge. Without soil, rain would run into rocky cracks, wearing them into bigger caves and tunnels.

Those feet were made for walking...?

Only a few types of trees can survive without soil. They grow from the thin dust in cracks on rocky mountainsides. Nearly all other trees need soil. The tree's roots anchor it in the soil as well as take in nutrients and water. Without soil, tree animals, like monkeys, would have to walk more, and would get sore feet!

The amazing graze!

Sheep, cows, and many other farm animals eat grass, which grows in soil. Without farm animals, there would be much less meat to buy. Wild animals such as deer also eat grass and leaves. Without them, hunting animals, such as lions and tigers, would run out of food, too. Food chains, and the whole web of life would be unbalanced.

Sweat and soil

If there were no soil, it might be possible for us to make our own. We might grow flowers, fruits, and vegetables in tubs of sand or gravel. But we'd have to keep adding plenty of water and fertilizers containing minerals and nutrients, or the plants would soon shrivel up and die. Natural soil has these nutrients, and does not need a lot of extra care.

Going underground

Rabbits, mice, shrews, foxes, badgers, prairie dogs, and hundreds of other creatures dig their homes in the soil, making tunnels and chambers. Moles live underground almost all their lives, digging through the soil and eating worms, slugs, and other small soil creatures. If the soil ever disappeared, they would need a lot of help to tunnel, as they would be faced with the hard rock beneath!

WHAT IF FOSSIL FUELS RAN OUT?

There are three main groups of fossil fuels: various types of coal and anthracite; gasoline, diesel, and kerosene made from crude oil (petroleum); and natural gas. They are all made from the rotted, fossilized remains of plants and animals which lived millions of years ago. If they ran out, millions of cars, trains, planes, factories, and power stations would come to a standstill. The bad news is that fossil fuels are running out, far faster than they are made by natural processes.

Alternative energy

Fossil fuels can be made into electricity, which is our favorite energy form – efficient and easy to transport along wires. The best ideas for the future are "natural sustainable" forms of energy (below). These don't damage or pollute the environment as much as fossil and nuclear fuels. They will also last because, in one way or another, they're all driven by the Sun's energy.

Nuclear energy is efficient, but it produces dangerous radio-activity that lasts for thousands of years.

Solar (Sun's) energy can be turned into electricity. It is most worthwhile in hot places.

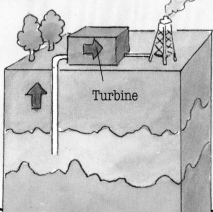

Geothermal energy (heat from deep underground) is easily available in some places, such as hot springs and geysers.

Turbine

Three, two, one... We have lift-off?

No we don't – rocket fuels are mostly made from crude oil (petroleum), so we couldn't launch any more satellites. How about a flying wing covered with solar cells? These convert sunlight into electricity, which is stored in batteries and turns the propellers. Flying far above the clouds, the solar wing could replace satellites.

Reasons for recycling?

To save all kinds of resources. Recycling stops us digging up so much of the Earth for ores and raw materials. It saves the fuels that we use to convert the ores and raw materials into metals, plastics, and other finished products. It stops us from cutting down more trees to make new paper. Recycling is good for the environment. So do it!

A solar car will turn sunlight into electricity for its electric motors. Quiet, clean, non-polluting – great!

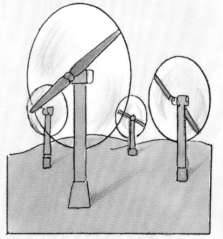

Wind energy is created as the Sun heats the air. It will last for a long time, but rows of modern wind turbines needed to harness the energy are expensive, noisy, and spoil the countryside.

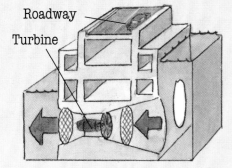

Roadway
Turbine

Tidal energy harnesses the sea's movements caused by the Moon's gravity. Wave energy comes from wind, but the barrages needed disrupt shore and sea life.

Hydroelectricity is created by water flowing through turbines, driving generators. Efficient and clean, it can drown valleys.

The holes, or thin parts of the ozone layer, are mainly over the North and South Poles.

WHAT IF THE OZONE HOLE GETS WORSE?

Ozone is an invisible gas, a form of oxygen. It forms a layer high in our atmosphere, which blocks out harmful ultraviolet (UV) rays from the Sun. Some chemicals that industries put into the air are destroying the ozone layer. If more UV rays get through, they could cause more sunburn, cancers, and skin diseases. We can't sew up the ozone hole, so we must stop releasing these ozone-destroying chemicals, now! In fact, we should take more care of our Earth altogether.

FACTOR 30

How can we kill pests without using pesticides?

Weevils, gall wasps, aphids, locusts, and many other insect pests damage farm crops, as do plant and fungal pests like rusts and mildews. We control them by spraying factory-made chemical pesticides. But these can get into the rivers and soil and may harm wildlife. We should try harder to use natural pest controllers, such as ladybugs that eat aphids, and parasitic wasps that lay their eggs in locusts. However, we must always be very careful. When cane beetles ate the sugar cane crops in north-east Australia, people brought a beetle-eating toad from South America as a natural pest controller. But the toad settled in so successfully, that it has now become a major pest itself.

The global greenhouse

Gases in the atmosphere, such as carbon dioxide, retain just the right amount of heat to enable life to exist on Earth. This is called the *greenhouse effect*. Now we burn more fuels, releasing more carbon dioxide, causing the Earth's temperature to rise. It could melt polar ice caps, raise sea levels, and cause flooding.

Why are rainforests so important?

Because they are home to millions of awesome trees, beautiful flowers, and exciting animals! And they also refresh the air. All plants live by the process of photosynthesis. They catch light energy from the Sun and use it to live and grow. During this process, they take in carbon dioxide from the air, and give out oxygen – the reverse of what we do when we breathe. The forests also affect the weather and global patterns of climate! Burning the great forests upsets the global greenhouse.

Now, some reflected heat is trapped due to greenhouse gases.
More heat is trapped

Before, some reflected heat escaped into space.

Some heat is reflected

Sun's rays

Some rays reach surface

THE CRAZY WORLD OF

THE HUMAN BODY

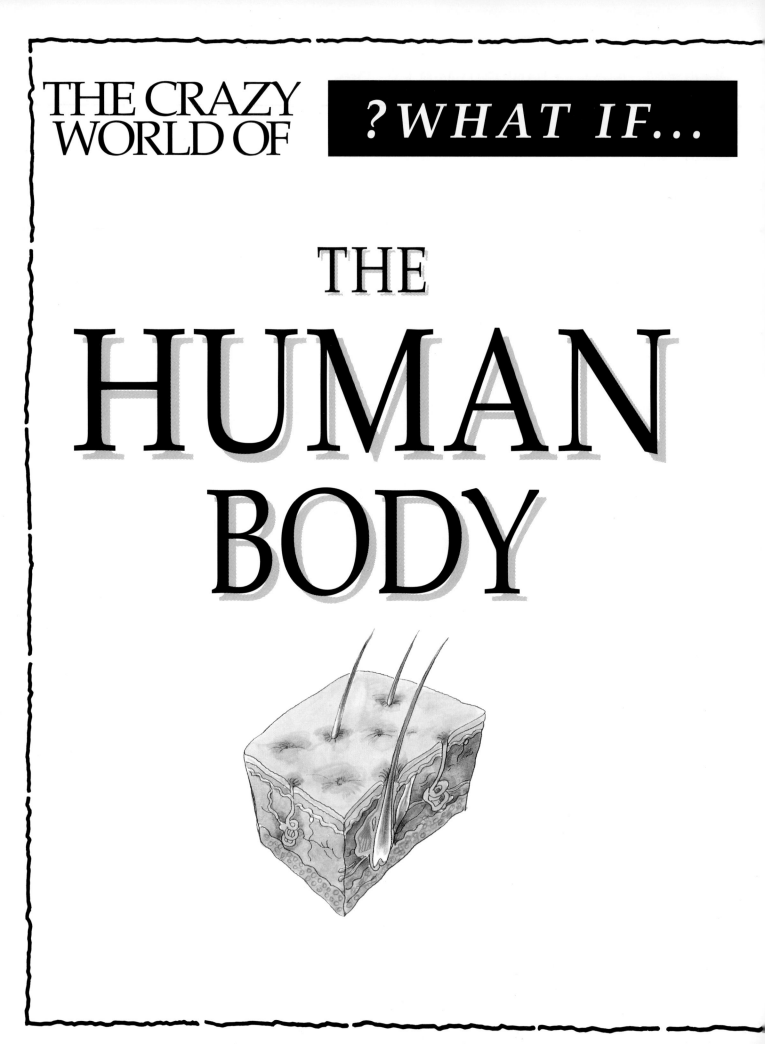

CONTENTS

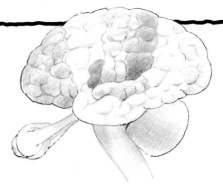

90 What if we had no skin?

92 What if we had no muscles?

94 What if we had no bones?

96 What if we stopped breathing?

98 What if your heart stopped beating?

100 What if we had no nose or mouth?

102 What if the body had no stomach?

104 What if we only ate lettuce?

105 What if we had no lymph?

106 What if we were brainless?

108 What if we had no eyes?

110 What if we could hear like a bat?

112 What if people didn't have sex?

114 What if we grew as fast as a whale?

116 The body systems

Hair

Epidermis

Sweat pore

WHAT IF WE HAD NO SKIN?

Skin does so many vital jobs that you'd notice right away if it weren't there. Of course, the body would look dramatically different! Without skin, the fatty and fleshy layers underneath would be exposed. Dust and dirt would stick, and body fluids and salts would leak away. The body surface might become scaly, like a lizard! The body would have no protection against knocks and bumps. It would also be exposed to cold winds or the sun's heat – so you might freeze, or roast!

Sweat gland

Dermis

Hair root

Nerve

Sebaceous gland

An average piece of skin is ¹/₁₀ inch thick. The upper layer of skin, the epidermis, resists wear by replacing itself. Below is the thicker dermis.

Don't be thick skinned...

Much thicker skin would protect and insulate you better. But thicker skin has more folds and creases, so we might look like elephants or rhinos! Our skin would also weigh more than usual, so it would be like wearing a very heavy, stiff, cracked leather overcoat, even in bed!

...or thin!

Thin skin might look smooth and sleek, but it would protect the body less against too much heat or cold. And even small bumps could hurt and cause large cuts and bruises.

A skinless body would show layers of muscles, blood vessels, and fat.

Why do we get suntanned?

Skin exposed to lots of sunlight makes more pigment called *melanin*, a dark-brown substance that colors the skin. It shades the skin and parts beneath from UV light and the skin becomes darker. We call this process suntanning. The ultraviolet (UV) rays in sunlight can harm living things. If fair skin is exposed to too much hot sun at once, it will turn red and burn.

Does our skin need its natural oils?

Yes! The skin's mix of natural oils and waxes, called *sebum*, comes from tiny sebaceous glands just under its surface. Sebum may cause pimples, but it is mainly helpful. It makes the skin softer, more supple, and more water-resistant. Otherwise, it would crack like an old boot, and soak up water in the bath like soggy cardboard!

Why does skin look old?

As skin ages, certain fibers in the dermis break down. Skin then loses its stretchy, elastic texture, and lines and wrinkles start to appear.

Hot under the collar!

If you didn't sweat, the body could become very ill with heatstroke! You sweat to lose excess heat in very warm weather, or if your muscles are very active. The skin's three million tiny sweat glands ooze watery sweat (perspiration) onto the surface. As it dries, it draws warmth away from the body. The blood vessels widen too, and lose extra heat, which makes you look red and flushed. Dogs, however, hardly sweat. They lose excess heat through their breath and tongue by panting!

WHAT IF WE HAD NO MUSCLES?

You could not tell anyone that you had no muscles, since you would not be able to talk – or move your head, or your arms or legs. In fact, you could not make any movements at all. Muscles power all body actions and motions, from jumping and lifting heavy weights, to smiling and blinking. These movements include breathing with the chest muscles, and the beating of the heart (by the muscles that make up its walls). So, a body without muscles would be quiet and still, and very soon, lifeless.

Could we be any stronger?

Almost anyone can build up muscle strength, by doing plenty of exercises and by eating nourishing foods. But human muscles have a size limit. Our close cousin, the gorilla, has the same number of muscles as we do, but many of them are naturally much larger and stronger. A large male gorilla is stronger than ten ten-year-old children.

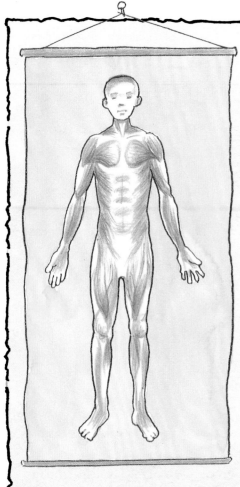

Hundreds of muscles
The body has three main types of muscles. The ones we often think of as muscles are skeletal muscles, shown on the chart above. There are more than 600 skeletal muscles all over the body, making up about two-fifths of the total body weight. The other types are visceral muscles, found internally, as in the stomach and intestines, and the cardiac muscle, found only in the heart.

No orbicularis oculi muscle (eyelids) = no blinking

No orbicularis oris muscle (lips) = no speaking

No intercostal muscles (between ribs) = no breathing

No cardiac muscle (in heart) = no heartbeat

Two muscles bend and straighten the elbow. As one pulls and shortens, it bulges in the middle. The other relaxes and stretches.

Triceps pulls back of forearm bone.

Can our muscles pull and push?

A single muscle can only get shorter, or contract, and pull the bone it is anchored to. It cannot push, like pistons in a bulldozer. So, many body muscles are in opposing pairs. One pulls the body part one way; the other pulls it back again. If muscles could push as well, you'd need fewer and would be thinner.

Biceps pulls front of forearm bone.

Pulling a muscle

Skeletal muscles are under the conscious control of the brain. You order them to pull. Nerve signals move from the brain along nerves called motor nerves, to the tiny myofibers that make up each muscle. The signals flow into the fibers and make them shorten. If these muscles worked when they wanted, body movements would be random and uncoordinated. You'd be a real jerk!

Nerve signals

Motor nerve

Muscle fiber contracts.

Nerve-muscle junction

Do we need our smallest muscle?

Yes! The stapedius is attached to the stapes (stirrup bone), which carries sound vibrations to the inner-most ear. With loud noises, the stapedius contracts to lessen them and so protects the delicate inner ear. Pardon?

WHAT IF WE HAD NO BONES?

Your body would fall down like a heap of jelly! Bones are tough and stiff, and there are 206 of them in the skeleton. They form the body's strong inner supporting framework. They hold up the softer parts like muscles, nerves, and blood vessels. Bones also protect delicate inner parts like the brain, heart, and lungs. Animals without skeletons or shells, such as slugs and worms, cannot grow very big or they'd flop over.

What's the point of a joint?

Without joints you'd be totally stiff and rigid. You couldn't walk or talk, or make any other movements – except swivel your eyes to look around, and then fall over!

Each bone is inflexible, but most bones are linked by flexible joints, so they can move in relation to each other. The amount of movement depends on the design of the joint. In the backbone, wrists, and ankles, lots of small movements between many bones add together to create lots of overall flexibility.

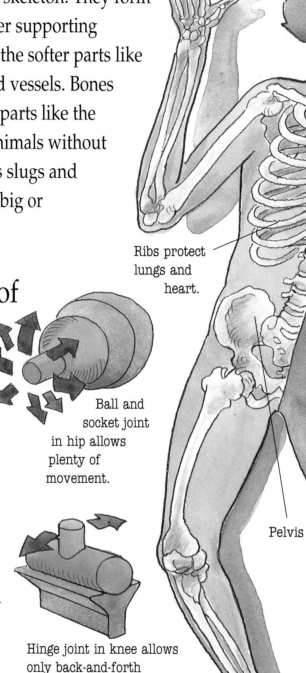

Skull protects brain.

Ribs protect lungs and heart.

Backbone

Ball and socket joint in hip allows plenty of movement.

Hinge joint in knee allows only back-and-forth movement, but is very strong.

Pelvis

Sliding joint between ankle bone allows limited movement.

94

Can bones be on the outside of the body?

Yes! Animals like insects, crabs, and spiders, have an exoskeleton – a skeleton on the outside, not the inside. An exoskeleton is a strong body casing that encloses the soft inner parts. It would protect us against bumps, cuts, and other damage. But compared to our lightweight endoskeleton of bones, it would be so heavy that we'd be unable to walk!

Hard outer bone layer

Softer, spongy inner bone layer

Bone marrow makes new red cells for the blood at the rate of more than one million every second!

Jellylike bone marrow

A boneless body would flop in a heap, like chunks of meat at the butcher's!

What is bone marrow?

Bone marrow makes microscopic red and white cells for the blood. Red cells carry vital oxygen (absorbed by the lungs from breathed-in air) all around the body. White cells fight germs and disease. These cells live for days or weeks. The marrow makes new ones to replace those that die. Without bone marrow, the body would turn pale, catch lots of illnesses, and die.

Do we have as many neck bones as a giraffe?

Well, er… yes, we do! Most mammals, from elephants and giraffes, to humans and horses, to mice and shrews, have roughly the same number of bones in their skeletons. But the individual bones are different shapes and sizes. You have seven neck bones, called *cervical vertebrae*. So does a giraffe – but its neck bones are, of course, much longer!

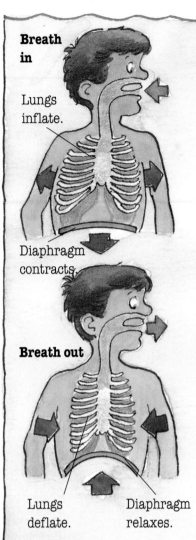

Breath in

Lungs inflate.

Diaphragm contracts.

Breath out

Lungs deflate.

Diaphragm relaxes.

WHAT IF WE STOPPED BREATHING?

For a few seconds, this does not matter – people hold their breath to swim under-water. But not breathing for longer than a minute or two is dangerous, as the body needs oxygen to live. Lungs breathe in air, absorb the gas oxygen from it, and pass the oxygen to the blood. This carries oxygen to all body parts. No breathing means no fresh oxygen, and when that happens, you don't last long!

Air in

Windpipe

Lungs

Ribs

The respiratory system takes oxygen from the air into the body.

Diaphragm

Heart

Could a mermaid live underwater?

No. She would drown! A mermaid has the upper body of a woman, so she'd need to breathe oxygen from air into her lungs. (That's assuming you believe in mermaids!)

How do fish stay alive?

A fish doesn't have lungs like we do. A fish has gills on either side of its head. They look like deep-red feathers, filled with blood. Gills do the same job as our lungs – take in oxygen. But they are designed to absorb oxygen which is dissolved in water, not gaseous oxygen from the air.

Low-oxygen water out through gill slits

Gills under gill cover

Oxygen-containing water in through mouth

Blowhole

Mouth

The dolphin's nostrils are on
its head, and are known as
the blowhole. To breathe,
it only has to poke this
part above the
water's surface.

Spiracles

Swimming with the dolphins

If we were like dolphins, we'd be able to blow
with amazing force, but we'd also have our
nose on top of our head! Dolphins and whales
are mammals, so they have lungs and breathe
air, like we do. They must
surface regularly for fresh air.

Could we breathe like insects do?

No. We'd need lots of holes
down the sides of our bodies!
Insects have these instead of
lungs. The holes are called
spiracles. They open into the trachea, a system of
body-wide hollow tubes. Fresh air seeps into
them, and stale air seeps out.

What has lots of pages but no words?

Book lungs! These actually exist in nature.
They aren't covered with words, but they do
have "pages" – lots of thin sheets, with a
large surface area. These sheets maximize the
area available for absorbing
the oxygen from the surrounding air.
One group of animals that have
these lungs is spiders. Their book
lungs are located in the lower
rear of their bodies, out of
harm's way.

Microscopic
water
creatures like
amoeba absorb
oxygen
through entire
body surface.

1 Blood into atria (upper chambers)

2 Through valves into ventricles

3 Muscular walls squeeze hard.

4 Blood into main blood vessels; new heartbeat begins

WHAT IF YOUR HEART STOPPED BEATING?

You would not be sitting there! If someone's heart stops beating, emergency medical help is needed. Without a beating heart to pump blood through our blood vessels, blood would not flow around the body. So, vital organs would not get their supplies of oxygen and energy-containing nutrients, which the blood carries to them. The brain, in particular, is very sensitive and without oxygen would be damaged in minutes.

Plastic pump
An artificial heart is made of metal and plastic. It is powered by high-pressure air.

What's the value of a valve?

Valves in the heart and main veins let blood move only in the correct direction. Without them blood would slosh back and forth, without direction, and fresh blood could not reach every part of the body.

Heart

Vessels called arteries carry blood away from heart.

Veins carry blood back to heart.

Back-pressure closes valve.

Normal pressure opens valve.

Does our heart beat as fast as a mouse's?

We'd feel very odd if it did. Our usual heart (pulse) rate is 60-80 beats per minute. A mouse has a heart rate of 500 or more! This is quite natural. Smaller animals have smaller hearts that beat faster, because they use up energy faster. An elephant's heart rate is only 20-25 per minute, and a blue whale's is less than 10!

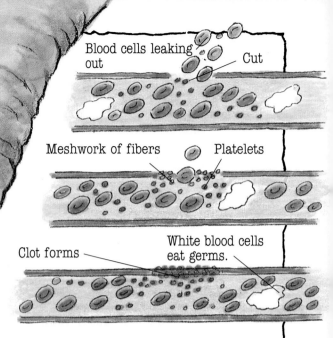

Blood cells leaking out — Cut

Meshwork of fibers — Platelets

Clot forms — White blood cells eat germs.

Smart clots

If our blood didn't clot, it would keep flowing from a cut for a long time. With a big cut, a lot of blood may be lost and there would be a risk of bleeding to death! Blood clots to seal a wound and help it heal, prevents blood from leaking out, and germs from getting in. Chemicals from the liquid part of blood combine with substances from microscopic blood cells, called *platelets*, to form a network of tiny fibers. These trap more cells, and a sticky clot builds up to seal the leak.

Can blood be green?

If it were you'd probably have two pincers and eyes on stalks, and be a lobster! Not all animals have red blood. In some snails it's blue, and in some worms it's yellow. Your blood's red color is due to the substance hemoglobin in billions of microscopic red blood cells. Oxygen from the lungs sticks to it and gets carried around to all body parts.

Giving blood

If you lost a lot of blood you'd need a blood transfusion. This means receiving fresh blood which is donated in small batches by other people, and kept in cold storage. A healthy human body should contain 8 pints (4-5 liters) of blood.

WHAT IF WE HAD NO NOSE OR MOUTH?

A fly tastes with its feet, and sucks up food with its mouthparts.

Incisors cut food like chisels.

Canine teeth rip food like little spears.

You would not be able to annoy people, by sniffing or talking too much. But you'd be unable to smell lovely scents, or taste delicious foods. In fact, you would be unable to eat or even breathe, since the nose and mouth are the openings for air going into the lungs. The nose is designed to make the incoming air warmer, moister, and cleaner by filtering dust with its hairs. The mouth is designed to bite, chew, and swallow food.

Premolars and molars squash and grind food, like a press or masher.

Bitter

Sour

Salty

A snake smells with its tongue!

False teeth
Some people lose their teeth from decay or injury. The dentist makes dentures – false teeth – that fit over the gums.

A clean sweep!

If we didn't brush our teeth, old food and germs would collect on them and rot, producing acid chemicals. These eat away each tooth's outer covering of tough enamel, and the slightly softer layer below, dentine. The tooth would develop holes, decay, and be very painful!

Crown

Cavity

Enamel

Dentine

Gum

Root

Nerves detect pressure and pain.

Jawbone

The sweet smell of...

If we had no sense of smell, we wouldn't have to smell horrible things, like exhaust fumes, or stagnant water from a polluted pond, or an unwashed person! But think of all the lovely scents we'd miss, like perfumes, flowers, and foods. Also, we might not be able to detect if food has gone bad and smells like rotten meat. Smells like this can tell us important information. A dog has a much better sense of smell than we do, and just by sniffing a place or object, can tell if a particular person has touched it!

A hard act to swallow!

Saliva is the watery substance (spit) made by six small glands around your face. It pours into your mouth as you eat, to make food moist and soft, and easier to chew and swallow. Saliva also contains natural chemicals called *enzymes* that start to digest the food. If you had no saliva, food would be very dry and hard to chew. How would you manage to eat cookies or crackers?

Tongue surface is roughened by small pimple-like projections called papillae.

Sweet

How tasteless?

Without taste buds, ice cream and chips would be tasteless! Flavors are detected by microscopic clusters of cells, called *taste buds*, on your tongue. You have about 8,000 taste buds which detect four main flavors – sweet at the tongue's tip, salty along the front sides, sour along the rear sides, and bitter at the back.

WHAT IF THE BODY HAD NO STOMACH?

You'd eat lots of small meals throughout the day, and probably at night, too! The stomach is like a balloon – a stretchy storage bag that expands as it fills up with food and drink from a meal. It squeezes and squirms to squash the food to a pulp, and mixes it with powerful acids and digestive chemicals made in its own lining. The result is a semi-digested soup that, over several hours, trickles into the intestines. Here the food is digested completely into nutrients. These are absorbed into the body for energy, growth, repair, and maintenance.

Monkey business

If you ate like the proboscis monkey you'd have a huge belly, which might make up half your whole body weight! This monkey only eats leaves such as mangrove leaves that are not very nutritious, so it has to eat so much that its stomach is jammed full.

The gullet (esophagus) – takes food from mouth to stomach.

Bile in the gall-bladder helps to digest fats.

The liver processes the nutrients from digestion, stores some for later, and makes bile fluid.

A full stomach holds more than one-half gallon of food and liquid. Its wall muscles make regular, strong motions.

The small intestine completes food digestion, absorbing nutrients into the blood flowing through its walls.

What if you had no kidneys?

You might save a few minutes by not going to the toilet. However, the kidneys are essential as they filter wastes and unwanted substances from the blood, and form them into watery urine. The bladder stores this urine until you have a convenient moment to get rid of it by urinating. If the kidneys were not there to do their job, the waste substances would build up in the blood. Within a few hours, they would poison the body.

Right kidney

Left kidney

Bladder

Pipe to outside (urethra)

The spleen stores nutrients and disease-fighting white cells, and recycles parts of the blood.

The pancreas makes juices called *enzymes* which attack the food.

WATER

Our water cycle

During digestion, lots of water is added to food, as digestive juices like acids and enzymes. The large intestine takes back most of it into the blood. Otherwise, you'd have to drink ten times as much!

Gone with the wind!

Digestion is a busy chemical process. Like other types of chemistry, it makes gases. These bubble throughout the stomach and intestines and eventually come out of your mouth or other end. It's very natural, but you can control when the gases come out, and whether they make a noise.

Straightening out your intestines

If your intestines were uncoiled, you would be about 33 ft (10m) tall, and incredibly thin! The small intestine is up to 23 ft (7m) long and the large intestine is about 5 ft (1.5m) long. The human body has them coiled up inside the abdomen.

The large intestine absorbs water and minerals from the undigested foods, and stores the remains as feces.

WHAT IF WE ATE ONLY LETTUCE?

Human bodies have evolved over millions of years. They are designed to eat natural and varied foods, especially leaves, fruits, vegetables, nuts, and similar plant foods, and some meats. In the busy modern world, we may eat only a few types of foods, which have been prepared, precooked, and prepacked to save us time. This can be unhealthy. A wide variety of different foods supplies the body with the nutrients it needs. So too much of any food, even lettuce, can cause illness. Over-eating makes us overweight, more prone to heart and blood vessel diseases, joint aches, and other problems.

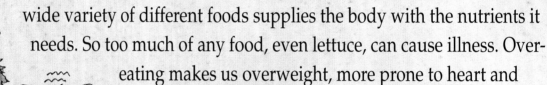

Sleeping beauty

Without sleep you would only last a couple of days before you started to get headaches, dizziness, sickness, confusion, and other problems. We all need regular rest and sleep, from 20 hours a day for a tiny new baby, to 7-8 hours for most adults. The most important fact is to be aware of the warning signs, and get as much sleep as you need.

Baring all!

If the weather were very warm, it might not matter to the body if we didn't wear clothes, but it might matter to other people! Anyway, if it's cold, you need clothes to keep you from shivering. Humans don't have thick fur like most mammals. So the body could not keep up its natural temperature. It would gradually suffer from hypothermia, and die.

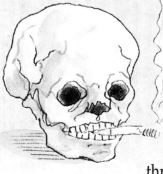

No smoking

The tars in tobacco smoke clog up the lungs and cause breathing problems and diseases. Smoking is also linked to cancers of the mouth, throat, and lungs. These can be deadly.

WHAT IF WE HAD NO LYMPH?

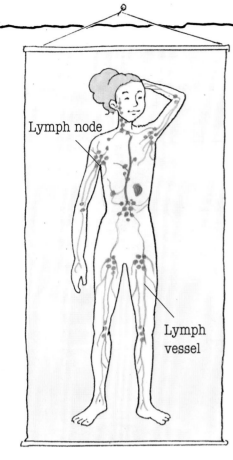

Lymph node

Lymph vessel

Cleaned, filtered lymph flows back to the blood.

Lymph fluid flows in from body cells and tissue.

If you had no lymph, you'd always be catching infections and suffering from diseases. Lymph is a pale fluid that flows through the body in tubes – lymph vessels – helping to spread nutrients and collect wastes. It also passes through lymph nodes or "glands." The smallest are the size of rice grains, the largest are as big as walnuts. They are full of microscopic white cells which clean the lymph and kill the germs that invade the body.

Germs are attacked and destroyed by antibody "rocket."

Some white-cell "spaceships" fire rockets – chemicals called antibodies – to destroy germs.

Some white-cell spaceships engulf and eat germs whole.

What do white blood cells do?

The body is under constant attack from germs floating in the air, in contaminated food and drink, and in dirt and soil that might get in through a cut. White cells go around the body, killing and eating germs, and constantly fending off the attack.

Cleaning up

If you didn't wash, dirt and germs would build up on your skin. You would smell and your skin would develop pimples. The dirt might also get onto your food and give you food poisoning!

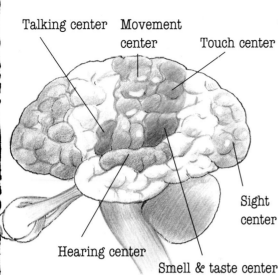

Talking center Movement center Touch center

Sight center

Hearing center

Smell & taste center

WHAT IF WE WERE BRAINLESS?

A brainless body would be unable to remember, imagine, think, talk, eat, even move or breathe. The brain is the control center of almost every bodily process. It is wired into the body by the spinal cord inside the backbone, and by dozens of long, thin nerves reaching every body part. Tiny electrical nerve signals pass along the nerves, keeping the brain informed and in charge.

What is it like to be senseless?

We would live in silent darkness, knowing nothing about our surroundings! The body finds out about the outside world by its main senses – eyes for sight, ears for hearing, nose for smell, tongue for taste, and skin for touch.

3 Nerve signals pass through reflex loop.

4 Nerve signals go down to muscle and make leg kick.

2 Nerve signals travel to spinal cord.

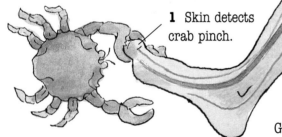

1 Skin detects crab pinch.

Goose's brain

Don't be a birdbrain!

If we were, we wouldn't realize it! Birds are not as self-aware as we are. But we'd know amazing things, like how to fly, build a nest, and navigate south for the winter.

Do our nerves work as fast as a squid's?

Different nerves in the body send signals at speeds from 400 ft (120m) per second. Squid have some nerves made of very thick fibers (giant axon) to carry signals more rapidly. With these, you could think and react really fast!

How big is your brain?

The main "thinking" part of your brain is its wrinkled, grooved surface, the cerebral cortex. Ironed flat, it's bigger than a large pillowcase, and about as thin. But you'd have to fold it back up to fit it in the skull!

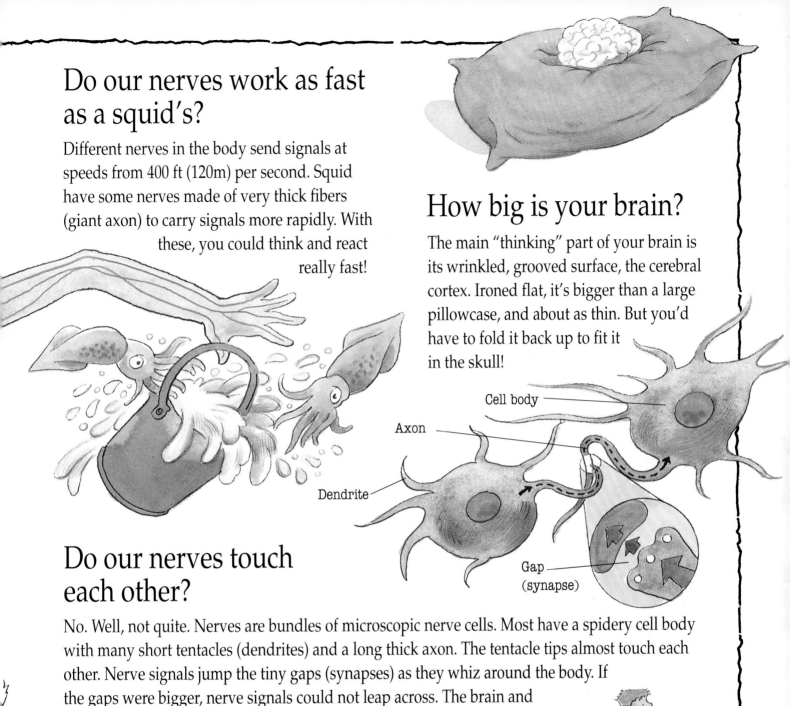

Cell body

Axon

Dendrite

Gap (synapse)

Do our nerves touch each other?

No. Well, not quite. Nerves are bundles of microscopic nerve cells. Most have a spidery cell body with many short tentacles (dendrites) and a long thick axon. The tentacle tips almost touch each other. Nerve signals jump the tiny gaps (synapses) as they whiz around the body. If the gaps were bigger, nerve signals could not leap across. The brain and nerve system would fail, and the body would be lifeless.

Dog's brain

WHAT IF WE HAD NO EYES?

We would not be able to look at this book, or our teachers... or the television! The eye detects patterns of light rays and turns them into tiny electrical signals, like a video camera. The signals go to the brain's visual centers, where they are processed and put together to create a detailed, full-color, continuously-updated view of the world around us. Some people are unable to see clearly, or at all and use other senses, such as hearing and touch, to find their way around and carry on successfully with their lives.

Sight of the bumblebee!

If our eyes were like bees' eyes, they'd be huge, cover most of the head, and be made up of hundreds of small eyelike units! Bees can see ultraviolet light, which our eyes cannot, so we could see patterns and lines in the sky, which could tell us where the sun was, even on a cloudy day. But the general view would be blurred, and we'd see fewer colors and details.

1 Light rays enter the eye through the clear, domed cornea at the front. This partly bends, or focuses, them.

2 The iris is a sheet of muscles that contract to change the size of the pupil, the hole in the middle.

3 Light rays go through the pupil which contracts in bright conditions, preventing eye damage.

4 The lens bends light rays to focus the picture, as well as turning the image upside-down.

Snails can't see detailed images, only shadows.

What's it like to be eagle-eyed?

The closest we can get to this kind of eyesight is to use binoculars! With our own eyes we can't see faraway things in incredible detail, like an eagle. This hunting bird could spot a rabbit 3 miles (5km) away, whereas you would be lucky to notice it at 0.6 mile (1km). But the eagle may not have such a good general view of the surroundings to see details across its whole area of vision, as we do.

5 The retina, a thin sheet of 130 million light-sensitive cells (rods and cones), changes light rays into nerve signals.

6 The nerve signals flash from the retina into the optic nerve, and then to the brain for sorting and analysis.

Rod

Cone

Cat's eyes

No animal can see in total darkness. But a cat's eyes are very sensitive to dim light, so they can see about five times better in the dark than we can. The normally slitlike pupil opens very wide, to let in as much light as possible. Also, a mirrorlike layer behind the retina, the tapetum, reflects light. This gives the retina two chances at detecting the rays. And it's why a cat's eyes shine in the dark!

WHAT IF WE COULD HEAR LIKE A BAT?

At nighttime, we would hear lots of squeaks. These are the noises made by other bats finding their way in the dark, using sound pulses and the pattern of returning echoes – *echolocation*, or sonar. We cannot normally hear the bat's sounds as they are ultrasonic (too high-pitched for our ears to detect).

Cochlear nerve
(hearing signals)

Vestibular nerve
(balance signals)

The semi-circular canals help with balance.

2 Sound waves go along the ear canal and hit the flexible eardrum at the end, making it vibrate.

Eardrum

Anvil

Stirrup

Hammer

3 Vibrations pass from the eardrum along a set of three tiny bones, the hammer, anvil, and stirrup, to the cochlea.

4 Vibrations pass into the cochlea, shake tiny hairs, and send nerve signals to the brain.

Eustachian air tube

Can we hear as well as an owl?

Each animal's hearing is adapted to its lifestyle. For instance, the owl's ears are low on the sides of its head, hidden by feathers. They are incredibly sensitive to tiny sounds in the quiet of night. The owl can pinpoint the position of a mouse on the ground, as it swoops in for the kill.

1 Sound waves are vibrations of molecules in air. These vibrations spread out like ripples on a pond.

Keeping an ear to the ground!

Human ears are located on the head with the other main sense organs – the eyes, nose, and tongue. Some insects have eardrum-type flaps for hearing, on other parts of their bodies. For example, the grasshopper listens to its neighbors chirping with ears which are on its knees!

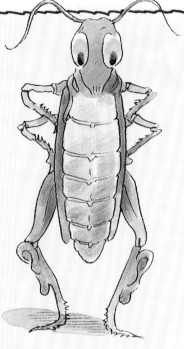

The only way is up!

You know which way is up or down, partly due to your sense of balance. The chambers and semi-circular canals deep inside your ears are filled with fluid and sensitive cells with micro-hairs in them. These detect gravity and any head movements. So you usually know which direction you are moving in, and how fast you are moving.

Your eyes can also see the ground below, the sky above, and upright walls, doors, and trees. All this helps you to keep your balance, otherwise you might wobble and fall over.

Ear-ear!

Many animals lack ears, such as the billions of worms in the soil and starfish in the seas, yet they survive very well! Worms cannot hear airborne sound waves, but they can sense vibrations in the ground. Water animals, like starfish, do not need to detect airborne sound waves, either. However, many have sensory parts to detect vibrations, ripples, and currents in the water.

WHAT IF PEOPLE DIDN'T HAVE SEX?

The human species would soon die out! If an alien space creature came to Earth, it would notice that there are two main kinds, or sexes, of human body – male and female. This is the same as in most other animals, from whales to fish, and eagles to ants. The male and the female mate together (have sex) to reproduce (make babies). A few animals, especially simple microscopic ones, can reproduce without mating. They divide into two offspring (right). This is asexual reproduction.

Animal magnetism

In some animals, such as frogs or fish, the males and females seem the same, but only to us. The animals themselves can tell the sexes apart. Sometimes it's by behavior – the male or female does a courting dance or takes up a certain body posture. It may be the different mating calls and songs they sing, or even the scents and smells they give off which show a difference.

The male body
An average adult male is taller, stronger, and hairier than a female. He has broad shoulders, narrow hips, a deeper voice, and facial hair. But there are many variations.

The male parts

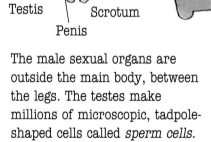

Sperm tube

Sperm

Testis   Scrotum
      Penis

The male sexual organs are outside the main body, between the legs. The testes make millions of microscopic, tadpole-shaped cells called *sperm cells*.

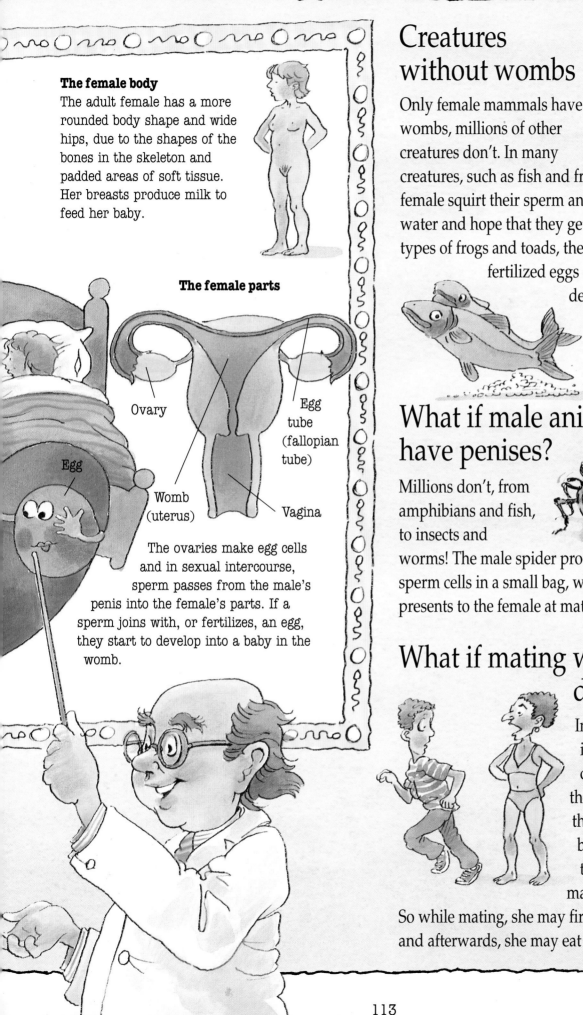

The female body

The adult female has a more rounded body shape and wide hips, due to the shapes of the bones in the skeleton and padded areas of soft tissue. Her breasts produce milk to feed her baby.

The female parts

Ovary

Egg tube (fallopian tube)

Egg

Womb (uterus)

Vagina

The ovaries make egg cells and in sexual intercourse, sperm passes from the male's penis into the female's parts. If a sperm joins with, or fertilizes, an egg, they start to develop into a baby in the womb.

Creatures without wombs

Only female mammals have wombs, millions of other creatures don't. In many creatures, such as fish and frogs, the male and female squirt their sperm and eggs into the water and hope that they get together. In some types of frogs and toads, the female gathers the fertilized eggs on her back. They develop as tadpoles in skin pockets, and emerge as tiny froglets!

What if male animals didn't have penises?

Millions don't, from amphibians and fish, to insects and worms! The male spider produces his sperm cells in a small bag, which he presents to the female at mating time.

What if mating were very dangerous?

In most animals, it isn't. But in some creatures, such as the praying mantis, the female is much bigger and stronger than the male. She may be hungrier, too. So while mating, she may first bite his head off and afterwards, she may eat him up!

WHAT IF WE GREW AS FAST AS A WHALE?

Sperm
and egg
0 months

Instead of taking nine months to grow inside our mother's womb, we would only take a day! In the two months before it is born, a human baby grows by about 4.4 lb (2kg) in weight. In the same time, a baby blue whale in its mother's womb grows by 2 tons – one thousand times as much! The time when the baby grows in the womb is called *pregnancy*.

Baby at
1½ months

Most of the development of body parts and organs in the human baby happen early, in the first two months of pregnancy, when the body of the baby is still only 1 in (25mm) long.

Baby at
2½ months

Baby at
6½ months

Baby after nine months in the womb, ready to be born

The ever-changing human body

Some parts of the human body never stop growing. Your hair, fingernails, and toenails grow throughout life, although some of the hairs may fall out in later years. You have to trim or cut your hair and nails so they don't get too long or dirty. Your skin also grows all the time, since about 13 lb (5kg) of it is rubbed away each year by daily activity.

What happens as we grow up?

Loads of exciting things! You learn to laugh, cry, smile, move about, hold things, crawl, stand, walk, talk, draw, read, write, play games, and study English, math, science, and history. Of course, people are different. Some are good at certain things, like sports. Others aren't. As you grow up, you also learn about rules and laws, how to behave properly and stay out of trouble, how to eat healthily and keep clean, and how to make lots of friends – but hopefully no enemies. Many people find a partner and have their own children. Many get jobs. Older people might take it easy, or stay busy and active! Everyone has occasional problems and heartaches along the way. It's all part of growing up.

How long can we live?

The average age people reach in most western countries is around 70-80 years. Overall, women live about 3-5 years longer than men. There are very few people over one hundred. But how much living you do, and how much you pack into those years, is up to you. Humans live a long time, compared to most animals. Some insects like small flies have hatched, grown, mated, and died within twenty days. Yet some huge reptiles, like giant tortoises, may live to be over 120 years old.

A kangaroo is born early. It does most of its growth not in its mother's womb, but in her pouch.

115

THE BODY SYSTEMS

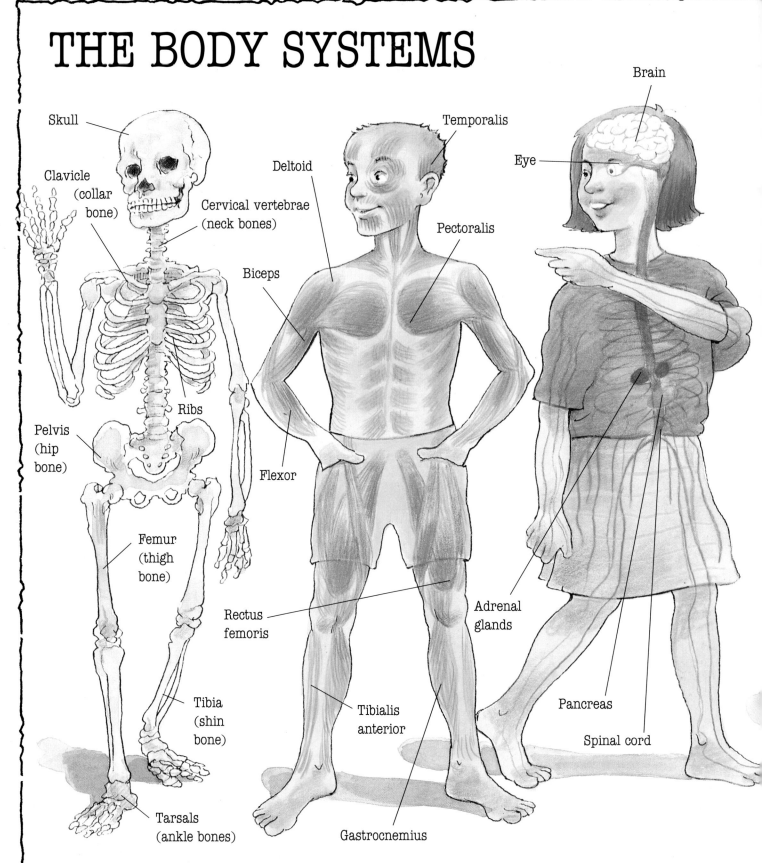

Skull

Clavicle (collar bone)

Cervical vertebrae (neck bones)

Biceps

Ribs

Pelvis (hip bone)

Femur (thigh bone)

Flexor

Rectus femoris

Tibia (shin bone)

Tarsals (ankle bones)

Temporalis

Deltoid

Pectoralis

Adrenal glands

Tibialis anterior

Gastrocnemius

Brain

Eye

Pancreas

Spinal cord

The Skeleton
206 bones provide a rigid frame-work moved by muscles and protect soft parts like the brain.

Muscles
Over 640 muscles pull bones, so you can move. Muscles are two-fifths of our total body weight.

Nerves, Senses, and Glands
The nerves and glands control the body's systems, using either chemical or electrical messages.

Jugular vein

Aorta (main artery)

Heart

Windpipe (trachea)

Saliva gland

Liver

Gullet

Lungs

Kidneys

Stomach

Ureter

Large intestine

Femoral artery and vein

Bladder

Anus

Small intestine

Circulation

The body's cardiovascular system circulates blood through the blood vessels pumped by the heart. The blood spreads oxygen and nutrients, and collects any of the body's waste products.

Respiration and excretion

In respiration, the lungs absorb oxygen from the air, and excrete, or get rid of, carbon dioxide. The kidneys excrete wastes by filtering them from the blood, to form urine.

Digestion

The mouth, gullet, stomach, and intestines break down food and absorb nutrients into the body. The pancreas makes digestive juices, and the liver processes and stores nutrients.

THE CRAZY WORLD OF

?WHAT IF...

GIRAFFES

CONTENTS

120 What if giraffes had short necks?

122 What if a leopard could change its spots?

124 What if a bat couldn't hear?

126 What if mammals laid eggs?

128 What if cows had no udders?

130 What if a lion had no pride?

132 What if a squirrel didn't store its nuts?

134 What if an elephant had no trunk?

136 What if a tiger had no teeth?

138 What if humans could grip with their feet?

140 What if sheep had no wool?

142 What if mammals had never existed?

WHAT IF GIRAFFES HAD SHORT NECKS?

Some do! The okapi is a type of giraffe found in the tropical rain forests of central Africa. Unlike its taller relative, the giraffe of the African plains, all of its food is within easy reach among the lush jungle vegetation.

As a result, it does not need the long neck of the plains giraffe. The tree branches of the African plains are found well above the ground, so the giraffe needs a long neck to stretch up and eat the leaves that can be over 19 ft (6 m) high. The giraffe's unique feature has evolved over years of evolution, so that it is now perfectly suited to its way of life.

Designed by committee

The odd shape of the giraffe, with its big head, long neck, long front legs, and short back legs, has often been described as an animal put together by a committee. However, the peculiar body has evolved naturally over time. The result may look odd, but it works.

Lookout post

Not only does the giraffe's tall neck allow it to reach the highest branches, it lets it see over long distances. High above the grassy plains, the giraffe can spot danger, such as a bush fire or a prowling hunter, or even new trees to eat, from several miles away.

Okapi

All creatures great and small

Just as the neck of the giraffe has developed over millions of years, so nature has created a whole host of different mammals. There are currently over 4,000 species of mammal, ranging from enormous whales to tiny mice, and from peaceful cows to aggressive tigers. Each of these has developed its own method of survival, involving a bizarre array of physical features. These include the hump of a camel, the stripes of a zebra, or the trunk of an elephant. All of these strange-looking features have evolved to help the animal survive in its environment.

The long and short of it

A giraffe, like all other mammals, including the okapi, has only seven vertebrae in its neck. However, these neck bones are greatly elongated (stretched), allowing the giraffe's head to stand way above the ground.

Giraffe

What if dinosaurs were still alive?

Then we would not be here! Mammals and dinosaurs first appeared at the same time, about 200 million years ago. However, it was the dinosaurs who were first to develop and rule the Earth. Mammals could not compete, and they had to be very small to survive. Then, mysteriously, the dinosaurs died out about 65 million years ago, and mammals were able to develop into their many and various forms (see above). If the dinosaurs were still here, then the largest mammal would probably be about the size of a cat.

WHAT IF A LEOPARD COULD CHANGE ITS SPOTS?

A leopard's spots are designed to break up its outline and keep it hidden, especially when it's crawling through the long grass, or lying on a tree branch. Many mammals have this type of camouflage – both the hunted and the hunters, including tigers. If these animals were brightly colored, or if they had strange patterns on their fur, they would stand out, and enemies could spot them at once!

Dappled deer

Adult red deer tend to graze in open areas. But baby red deer, called fawns, hide by lying still among ferns or heather, under a bush, or in a thicket. The sunlight shining through the leaves creates light and shadow below. So the fawn's coat has similar light and dark patches to conceal it in the dappled sunlight.

What if a polar bear had no fur coat?

Its naked, pinkish body would show up clearly against the white background of snow and ice. So the polar bear would have trouble trying to sneak up on seals to eat, and it would get very hungry. It would also be extremely cold. This is another job of a mammal's hairy coat – to protect against the cold (or heat, as in the case of a camel). The polar bear's fur coat is extremely thick and warm, as well as extra white. Without it, the bear would quickly freeze to death.

Stop blubbering!

All mammals have a layer of a soft, fatty substance just under the skin, covering the muscles and other inner parts. When this is very thick, it's called *blubber*. It makes the seal's body smooth and sleek, and acts as a store of energy should food ever get scarce.

However, its major role is as a wraparound blanket of fat to help the fur keep out the cold, especially when the animal is swimming in the icy seawater. Some seals can have a layer blubber that is more than 4 in (10 cm) thick.

Fur
Skin
Blubber
Muscle

Skinny seal
A blubberless seal would not only look very thin, it would very quickly freeze to death in the cold seas that it swims through.

What if mammals had spears and armor?

Some do – the porcupine has spines and the armadillo has armor-plating. The porcupine has normal mammal fur and also very thick, sharp-tipped, spearlike hairs growing from the skin. These are quills which are only attached loosely to the skin. The porcupine can flick its tail and throw off the quills into an unwary attacker's face.

The armadillo has a covering of small bone plates embedded in horny skin, with patches of tough skin and hairs between them. The plates hang down over the creature's head, sides, legs, and tail. When threatened, the armadillo can roll up into an armor-plated ball.

WHAT IF A BAT COULDN'T HEAR?

Clicks

Echoes

Bat sonar

The bat's sound pulses are so high-pitched that you or I couldn't hear them. However, a bat's hearing is so sensitive, it can hear these clicks and their echoes. The bat can find its way and catch its flying food even in complete darkness. The system is like radar, but with sound waves instead of radio waves. It's known as sonar or echolocation.

It would fly through the dark night – and crash into things! Mammals possess an amazing array of senses to detect the outside world. Hearing is only one of these. They are able to see in very poor light, smell the very faintest odors, taste an enormous variety of different foods, and detect touches and vibrations that are as light as a feather.

Dolphin sonar

Predatory members of the whale group, such as dolphins and killer whales, have a sonar system like the bat's (above). The sound pulses are concentrated, or focused, into a beam by a large lump in the forehead, the melon.

melon

What if whales could sing?

All whales make underwater sounds, varying from shrill clicks and squeaks and squawks, to haunting low moans and groans. Beluga and humpback whales are so noisy that their calls can be heard underwater more than 125 miles (200 km) away. The "songs" of a whale can last between 6 and 35 minutes, and are used by the whales to communicate with each other.

Nighttime eye-shine

If you've ever shone a flashlight into a cat's eyes, you will have seen that they appeared to glow in the dark. A cat's eye has a mirrorlike layer inside, the tapetum. Light rays come into the eye and some are detected by the light-sensitive layer, the retina. Others pass through the retina, bounce off the tapetum, and get sensed by the retina on the way out. This gives the eye two chances to detect light rays. Other nocturnal (nighttime) animals, such as opossums, have this too.

The pupil opens wider in dark conditions, to let in more light.

The retina detects light and turns it into nerve signals, which go to the brain.

The tapetum is a layer behind the retina. It reflects the light back onto the retina.

What if a lion had eyes on the side of its head?

It would leap at its prey, and probably miss! Most hunters, such as seals, cats, and foxes, have two forward-facing eyes at the front of the head. This gives them overlapping fields of vision (right), and allows them to judge distances well, for pursuit and pounce. Most hunted mammals, such as deer, zebras, and rabbits, have eyes on the sides of their head. Although this means that they can't judge distances well, it does give them a good overall view for spotting any predators that may be creeping up on them (right).

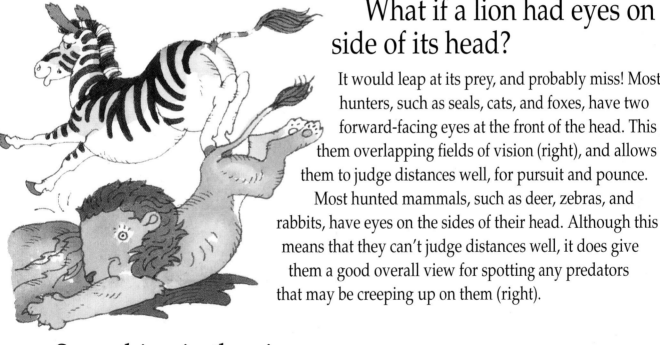

Something in the air

Dogs sniff everything, from the food they eat, to other dogs, especially when it is time to mate. The scent in the air enters the nose and attaches to an organ called the *olfactory bulb*. This is very large and very sensitive in a dog's nose. It then sends signals to the brain.

Olfactory bulb

WHAT IF MAMMALS LAID EGGS?

You would need very strong eggshells! Fortunately, very few mammals actually lay eggs in the same way as birds and reptiles. Those that do, such as the bizarre-looking duck-billed platypus, are called *monotremes*. Other mammals give birth to live young. Some, called *marsupials*, carry the young in a pouch, while the rest keep the immature baby within a part of their body called the *womb*. Here it can grow and develop.

This period of time when the baby mammal is inside the mother is called the *gestation period*. Its length varies greatly, depending on the size of the animal. The human gestation period is about 270 days. The Asiatic elephant can carry its young for an astonishing 760 days. However, the Virginian opossum is pregnant for as little as eight days!

Egg-cellent parents!

There are only three species of mammal that actually lay eggs. These are the duck-billed platypus (above), the long-beaked echidna (right), and the short-beaked echidna, which all live in Australasia. The duck-billed platypus usually lays two eggs in an underground den. These eggs are covered in a tough leathery shell to protect them.

After about ten to twelve days in the den, the babies hatch from their eggs and feed on milk. This is produced by special glands on the mother (see page 128).

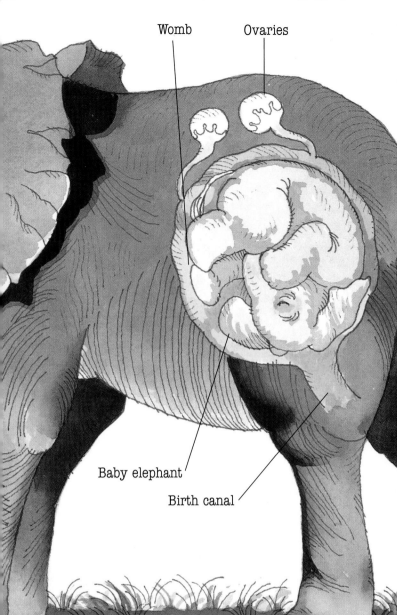

Womb   Ovaries

Baby elephant

Birth canal

Eggs without shells

Although most mammals don't lay eggs like birds or reptiles, they all (including humans) produce tiny, microscopic eggs from organs inside the female, called ovaries. After mating, these eggs may be fertilized with sperm from the male, and embed themselves into an area of the mother's womb. The baby grows here, protected from the outside world and fed by nutrients that pass from the mother's blood. These nutrients are passed from the mother to the baby through an organ called the placenta, and along the umbilical cord. Once the baby has developed enough, it is born. It passes from the womb, through the birth canal, and out into the world.

What if a kangaroo didn't have a pouch on its belly?

It would have to find some other way of carrying around its young. Kangaroos give birth to very immature, furless babies. The tiny creature has to crawl through its mother's fur, into the pouch, where it attaches itself to one of four milk teats.

The pouch is called a marsupium, and mammals that have this are referred to as marsupials. These include possums, opossums, koalas, kangaroos, and wombats.

WHAT IF COWS HAD NO UDDERS?

The udders of a cow hold the milk-producing glands, known as mammary glands. Mammals are the only animals to have these milk-producing organs to feed their young. The young cow merely has to suck on its mother's teats to be fed with a rich supply of nutrients. These are essential for the calf during the first months of its life. Without udders and teats, the young calves would starve, and we would be without milk to pour over our cereal in the morning!

Milk glands

Udders

What if we drank seal's milk?

We would get very fat indeed! The milk that different mammals produce varies greatly, depending on the needs of the young animal. Seals need to put on a thick layer of fat, called blubber, to keep them warm in the cold sea (see page 123). The milk that seal mothers produce is, therefore, very high in fat. Cow's and human's has only 4.5%, while seal's milk contains 53.2% fat – not very good if you're on a diet!

Bouncing delivery

When an infant kangaroo (joey) first reaches its mother's pouch after birth, it attaches itself to one of four teats (see page 127). The teat then swells and fixes the joey firmly within the pouch. It remains clamped to the teat for about two months, by which time the mouth has grown enough to release the joey. After another four months, the joey is old enough to leave the pouch, but it still continues to feed on its original teat, even climbing into the pouch when it needs a rest.

Meanwhile, another baby kangaroo may have been born. This, too, will have crawled into its mother's pouch and will be suckling on a different teat. Kangaroos can therefore carry two joeys in their pouch at the same time.

Feeding time

As the joey grows, the milk it drinks from the teat changes. At birth, the milk is very rich in nutrients, which decline as it gets older. With two babies feeding in the pouch, the mother will be producing two different types of milk!

What if baby mammals were left to fend for themselves?

They would become easy food for predators such as wolves, lions, and eagles!

Without any parents to take care of them, baby mammals would have to learn to hunt, hide, and forage in order to reach adulthood. Fortunately, mammal parents take more care of their young than any other animals, ensuring that plenty of them get to old age. The parents' first concern is to feed their young. This is done by supplying milk from the mother. They must also teach their babies how to find food, either by hunting or grazing.

As the young grow, the parents must also protect them from any predators that are after an easy snack. This doesn't mean that baby mammals are completely helpless. Some, like antelope, are able to run almost as soon as they are born.

129

WHAT IF A LION HAD NO PRIDE?

Solitary cats

Apart from the lion, all 34 other kinds of cats – from tigers to wildcats – are mainly solitary. They live and hunt alone. Only during the breeding season when a male and a female are together, and when a mother is with her cubs, do these cats have any company.

It would be very lonely. Lions are the only cats that live in groups, or prides. As with any group of animals, each of the lions has a different role. The females hunt for food and bring up the babies, or cubs. The males defend the females of the pride and the area of land where they live, called the *territory*, from rival males and other prides of lions.

Elephants on parade

When moving from place to place, elephants may walk in a long line, like soldiers on parade. The herd is led by the oldest female, or cow, the matriarch. The rest of the herd, including her sisters, daughters, and their babies, rely on her to find food and water.

Rival male

A fully grown male will leave his original pride. He will then wander alone for a while, then try to join another pride, so that he can mate with the females, and father offspring. But first he must challenge the pride's leader.

Leader of the pride

The chief male of the pride defends his females and territory fiercely. He fluffs up his mane to look large and strong, and growls loud and long. He tries to repel the rival by fright first. If this doesn't work, it may come to a real fight!

Female hunters

The older, experienced females are the pride's main hunters. They work together to chase and separate a herd of zebra and wildebeest, then they run down a young, old, or sick member. However, they will let the pride-leading male eat first.

Safety in numbers

Many large plant-eating mammals form herds with others of their kind. Sometimes they form mixed herds too, like zebra with wildebeest and gazelles. These herds can number from a handful to many thousands of animals.

There are many noses and pairs of eyes and ears that can detect any approaching danger. If one herd member spots trouble, it can warn the others. Should a predator approach too closely, the herd panics and runs. The hunter then finds it hard to single out one victim from the blur of bodies, heads, legs, and stripes that flash past very quickly.

Trooping baboons

The baboon is a type of monkey that spends much of its time on the ground. Baboons dwell in groups called *troops*, which can be subdivided into bands, clans, and family groups. The troops can number up to 250 baboons. These are based around the mothers and their children. There are a few males, and the biggest, most senior of these lead the troop from danger or defend it against predators, such as the leopard.

Lion cubs
Females with young cubs guard their offspring and feed them on mother's milk. However, danger may come with a rival male, which will kill any existing cubs if it takes over the pride so that its own can be reared.

Young males
The growing males stay with the pride, as long as they do not threaten the leading male. When they want to have any cubs of their own, then they must either challenge the leading male, or leave and take over another pride.

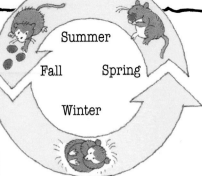

Summer

Fall Spring

Winter

WHAT IF A SQUIRREL DIDN'T STORE ITS NUTS?

The big sleep

Squirrels and many other small mammals sleep for long periods in winter, when the weather is cold and food is scarce. By going to sleep, they are able to slow down the speed at which their body works (see below) and so save energy. To prepare for winter, the mammal has to fatten itself up during fall, before it goes to sleep.

It might starve during the long winter months, when food is hard to find. Many mammals gather food during times of plenty, to hide away and keep, and eat when food is scarce. Squirrels collect fall nuts, such as oak acorns and hazel cobs, and bury them in the ground. Later, the squirrel is only able to find about one-quarter of the nuts it stored, but that's enough to see it through the winter months.

Life in the fast lane

Different mammals live to different ages. In general, bigger mammals live longer. They need the time to grow from a baby to full size. Small mammals, however, live their life faster. Their body processes, such as heartbeat and breathing, are quicker. A shrew's heart beats 800 times a minute, even when it is resting. An elephant's beats a mere 25 times a minute. All this activity and action mean smaller animals "wear out" and die sooner. A shrew aged six months is very old, whereas elephants may live to more than 70 years.

Gliding and flying

A few small mammals are capable of gliding and even flying. Flying squirrels and gliding possums can swoop, using a flap of skin between their legs, like the wings of a glider.

However, bats are the only mammals that can truly fly. During millions of years of evolution, the bat's arms have developed into wings. The long finger bones hold open a very thin, leathery wing membrane, which the bat flaps to stay in the air.

Membrane

Finger

Going underground

While some small mammals live in the trees, or swoop and soar through the sky, others have chosen to spend their lives underground. A mole tunnels by scraping and pushing aside the soil with its large, powerful, spade-shaped front paws. These have very big, strong claws, like the spikes of a pickax. The mole pushes up extra soil here and there, forming molehills. Tunnels radiate from a central nest, called the fortress.

This mammal spends most of its life underground, roaming its existing tunnels and digging new ones, to find food such as earthworms and soil grubs.

Working on the nightshift

Many small mammals, such as bats and rats, are active mainly when it is dark. These nighttime animals are called nocturnal. Other mammals, such as monkeys and squirrels, are active mostly by day. They are diurnal.

Night mammals usually have large eyes to see in the dark, keen noses to smell, extremely sensitive hearing to sense the slightest sound, and large whiskers to feel their way. Day mammals, like the bear, only need small eyes to see in the bright sunlight. If these daytime mammals went out in the dark, they would never be able to find their way.

WHAT IF AN ELEPHANT HAD NO TRUNK?

Trunk call

The hairy tip of the trunk is very sensitive to touch. The two holes are nostrils that lead to the long nose tube. Through this the elephant breathes and trumpets its calls. Muscles bend the trunk in any direction.

The long trunk is one of the main features of the animal, and it couldn't survive without it. The trunk is the nose and upper lip, that have joined together and grown very long. The elephant uses its trunk for many vital actions, especially eating and drinking. Without a trunk, this plant-eater would not be able to pick up grass and leaves to eat. It also uses the trunk to smell, breathe, feel, and to suck up water. If the elephant crosses a deep river, it can even use its trunk as a snorkel!

Sniffing and smelling

Elephants lift their trunks high to sniff the air for predators, fire, and other dangers, and to catch the scent of their herd and other creatures. They also smell food before eating it.

The daily grind

Long, thin, sharp, fang-shaped teeth are good for catching, killing, and ripping up meaty prey – but they are no good for chewing or grinding up leaves, grass, fruits, and other plant parts. Herbivores (plant-eaters) need wide, broad, fairly flat teeth to mash and pulp their food thoroughly. This is because plants are made from tough fibers that need to be broken down, so that a herbivore's intestines can extract the nutrients.

Feeding

The elephant has a short neck, so its head cannot reach down to the ground or up to the trees. But the trunk can. It curls around juicy grasses and leaves, rips them off, and stuffs them into its mouth.

Communicating

Elephants touch and stroke their fellow herd members, to greet them and keep up their friendships. They also trumpet and make noises with the help of their trunk. These forms of communication are very important to the herd.

Chewing the cud

Some mammals are able to swallow their food quickly, and then bring it up again to chew over slowly. They are called *ruminants*. They include cows, antelope, and llamas.

When the food is first swallowed it goes into the rumen, the first part of the four-chambered stomach (below). The animal can then bring up this half-digested food, called *cud*, to chew over more leisurely. The cud is then swallowed into the reticulum, and then into the intestines.

Drinking and bathing

The trunk's long nasal tubes allow the elephant to suck up enormous amounts of water. This can then be flung over its back when it wishes to cool off at a watering hole. Alternatively, the elephant may be thirsty, and then it will empty its trunk into its mouth to take a drink.

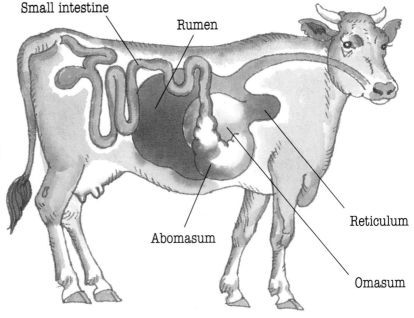

Small intestine

Rumen

Abomasum

Reticulum

Omasum

WHAT IF A TIGER HAD NO TEETH?

Carnassial teeth

It would soon go hungry and starve. The tiger uses its claws to catch and scratch prey. But it needs its teeth to deliver the deadly bites, and to slice the meat off the bones for eating. The tiger has two main kinds of teeth for these jobs. The long, sharp canines or "fangs" are at the front of the mouth. They stab, wound, and skin the victim, making it bleed, suffocate, and die.

The large, ridge-edged carnassial teeth at the back of the mouth come together like the blades of scissors when the tiger closes its jaws. These very strong teeth carve off and slice up the meat, and can even crunch gristle (cartilage) and soft bones.

Canine teeth

Purr-fect claws

A cat's claws are vital for its survival in the wild. With these incredibly sharp weapons, the hunter can slash, stab, and pin prey that will become its food. However, these deadly claws need to be kept razor sharp for the next kill. To ensure this, most cats can withdraw, or retract, their claws into sheaths in the toes.

This allows the cat to run, walk, and jump without scraping its sharp talons along the ground. It keeps them sharp, unbroken, and clean. It keeps them from getting blunt or getting tangled in twigs, grass, bark, and other things. When the cat needs its claws to climb a tree or to slash and pin its prey, it makes them stick out of the toes.

Claws indoors

The cat's claw is equivalent to your fingernail or toenail. But the claw can swing or pivot on its toe bone. A muscle in the lower leg pulls on a long, stringlike tendon that is attached to the bone and claw. This pulls the sharp claw out of its protective sheath.

Bone

Tendon

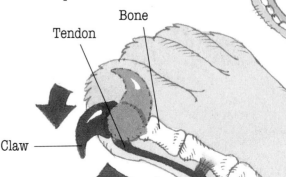

Claw

Plant-eating carnivore

When the giant panda of China was first discovered, it posed a problem to scientists. It has the sharp, fanglike teeth of a carnivore (meat-eater), and is indeed a close relative of the meat-eating raccoon. However, its diet consists almost solely of bamboo shoots. Even though it can eat meat, the panda chooses the young shoots of this type of grass. Unfortunately, bamboo is very low in nutritional value. As a result, it must spend nearly all of its time sitting around, lazily eating in order to consume enough to survive.

Highly-sprung hunter

The fastest hunter on land owes its speed to its flexible backbone. Without this powerful spring running along its spine, the cheetah would not be able to catch and kill the nimble prey that it hunts, such as gazelle and springbok.

As this big cat sprints, the spine flexes, stretching the body out, and allowing the legs to cover even more distance with each stride. This makes the cheetah the world's fastest runner, at over 60 mph (100 km/h).

As the cheetah's legs come together, the spine bends up in the middle.

As the cheetah extends its legs, the spine flattens and arches backward.

As a result the legs can stretch further apart, letting the cheetah run faster.

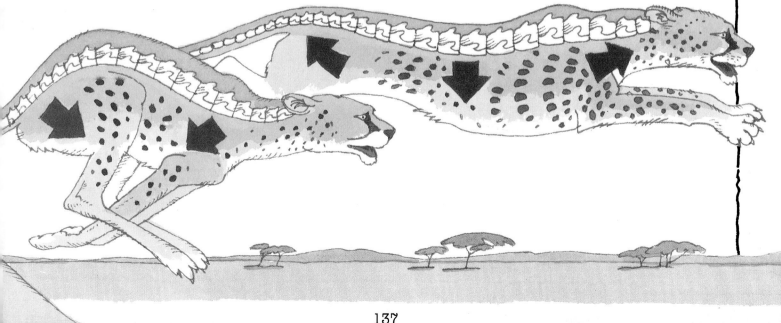

WHAT IF HUMANS COULD GRIP WITH THEIR FEET?

You could hang upside down from a tree, and do all kinds of other exciting activities. But you might not be able to run and jump so easily. Human feet are designed for walking, and human hands for holding. Our monkey and ape cousins spend most of their time in trees, so they don't need to walk. Instead, all their limbs can grip like hands. Some monkeys are even able to grip with their tails!

Orangutan

These great orange apes live in the densest, steamiest rainforests of Southeast Asia. They rarely come to the ground, and they can bend their legs at almost any angle from the body.

What if apes could stand upright?

One close cousin of the great apes spends most of its time upright. That's us! The true great apes, however, are not able to stand for long. The gorilla spends much of the day on the ground. It usually walks on all fours, on its feet and hand-knuckles. Males sometimes stand upright and charge, if they are threatened by an intruder. Chimps and orangutans can walk upright in order to carry things like fruit, sticks, or rocks. But they can only keep this up for short distances.

Gibbon

The gibbons of Southeast Asia are the champion tree-swingers. They hang from branches by their hooklike hands and powerful arms, and move by swinging from tree to tree with astonishing speed. Because of this, their arms are much longer and stronger than their legs.

Potto
This primate from Africa looks like a small bear. It moves very slowly through the trees.

Tarsier
The tarsier's huge eyes show that it comes out mainly at night. It can leap by its back legs to another branch 7 feet (2 m) away! It feeds on small animals and insects.

Flag-waving primate

Lemurs are primates from the large island of Madagascar, off the eastern coast of Africa. They can run across the ground or leap through trees with equal ease. When they aren't leaping about or searching for food, lemurs like to bask in the warm sun.

The ring-tailed lemur (below) signals to its troop by sight and smell. It waves its black-and-white, ring-patterned tail, like a flag. This is covered with a special scent that the lemur produces from glands on its shoulders.

Spider monkey
The spider monkey has a gripping tail, to help it move through the trees. Without it, the monkey might slip and crash to the floor.

What if apes could use tools?

Humans are not the only animals to use tools, many others use them as well. The great apes are tool-users, especially the chimp. It makes a tool by stripping the leaves off a twig, then pokes the twig into a termite mound, to dig out the termites for a snack. Animal tools are natural objects like leaves, stones, and twigs. They haven't figured out how to use any power tools, yet!

WHAT IF SHEEP HAD NO WOOL?

Humans have been using animals, such as sheep, cows, and pigs, for thousands of years. These domesticated mammals have been supplying us with meat, milk, and materials. If sheep didn't have any wool, then not only would they be cold, but we would not be able to use their fleece to make our woolen clothes.

Sheep's wool is sheared, washed, cleaned, and woven into clothes, rugs, and many other woolen products.

Mammal products

Mammals produce a wide range of products that humans use directly or convert into other substances. The milk of mammals such as cows, goats, and camels is made into butter, cheese, and yogurt. We eat the muscles, or red meat. We crush and melt bones and hard pieces into glues and fertilizers. Clothes and textiles are made from the wool (mammal fur) of sheep, goats, vicunas, rabbits, rodents, and many others.

Chamois leather is the skin of the chamois, a type of goat-antelope. It is very soft, flexible, and absorbent.

A-hunting we will go

Although hunting for sport takes place in many places throughout the world, several groups of people rely on hunting mammals to survive. For example, the Inuit (Eskimo) of the far north hunt whales, walruses, and seals for their meat, bones, and fur to make food, clothing, and utensils.

Bizarre pets

For as long as people have been using mammals for food, they have also been keeping them as pets. Since this time we have bred many different animals. Some of these were bred for their ability to work, such as sheepdogs, but now they are mainly for company or for show. The result has been some very strange-looking animals, such as the bulldog, whose nose is so short that it can only breathe through its mouth, the hairless sphinx cat, and the shaggy, rough-haired guinea pig.

Cows provide most of our ordinary leather. They also give us a lot of meat and make most of the milk that we drink.

Pigs yield many products, from meat to pigskin for shoes. They are used to make drugs and body organs for transplants.

Arks or prisons?

Zoos have become the center of debate between many groups of people. Some people believe that keeping wild animals captive in cages is cruel.

However, zoos can play a positive role in the conservation of many species. Conservationists can breed rare creatures such as the giant panda, golden lion tamarin, and rhinoceros, to release them back into the wild and save them from extinction.

Zoos have not always been successful in saving species. Some animals, such as the quagga from Africa and the thylacine from Australia, have become extinct, despite having some specimens kept in zoos.

Golden lion tamarin

Quagga

Giant panda

Rhinoceros

WHAT IF MAMMALS HAD NEVER EXISTED?

Mammals are quite recent arrivals on the world's stage. Although the first appeared 200 million years ago, they did not flourish until fifty million years ago. Since then they have come to dominate the world. If they had never been around, things would be very different.

Reptiles

Without mammals to compete with, the reptiles may well have recovered from the extinction of the dinosaurs, to rule the world again!

Arthropods

Spiders and scorpions are some of the oldest animals. Without mammals around to eat them and their food, there might be more arthropods around.

Amphibians

A lot of amphibians are eaten by mammals. Without them around, there would probably be a lot more frogs in the world.

Worms

Some mammals, such as moles and hedgehogs, feed on worms. Without mammals, worms could tunnel through the soil without being eaten.

What if there were no sea mammals?

Mammals are some of the largest creatures swimming throughout the waters of the world. Whales, dolphins, seals, and otters eat a massive amount of fish, krill, and other sea animals. Without mammals, there would certainly be a lot more fish around (especially because humans eat a vast quantity of fish every day!).

Other predators, such as sharks, would need to find alternative sources of food. However, there are plenty of other fish to eat. In fact, mammals only make up a small percentage of sea creatures, so if they had never existed, they wouldn't be missed all that much.

Insects
Some insects, such as mosquitoes, feed on the blood of mammals. Without mammals, they would have to find something else that they could eat.

Birds
Several species have been hunted to extinction by mammals, such as the diatryma and the elephant bird. If mammals had never been around, these birds could still be alive.

Mollusks
These creatures are incredibly successful and numerous in the sea, from sea snails to cuttlefish and squid. They provide food for both whales and dolphins. If they weren't eaten, they would be even more successful.

On top of the world

Without mammals there wouldn't be any humans. Scientists have pondered whether any other group of animal could produce a species as intelligent as ourselves. The favorites to fill the empty space might be the reptiles. They have already dominated the Earth once, during the reign of the dinosaurs. Some believe if they did not die out, then the world could be populated by highly intelligent, bipedal (two legged) lizards.

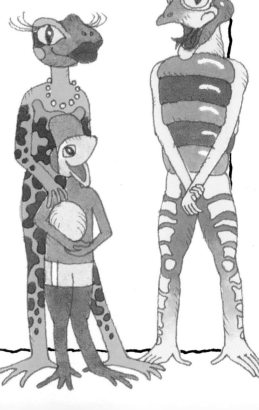

THE CRAZY WORLD OF

SHARKS

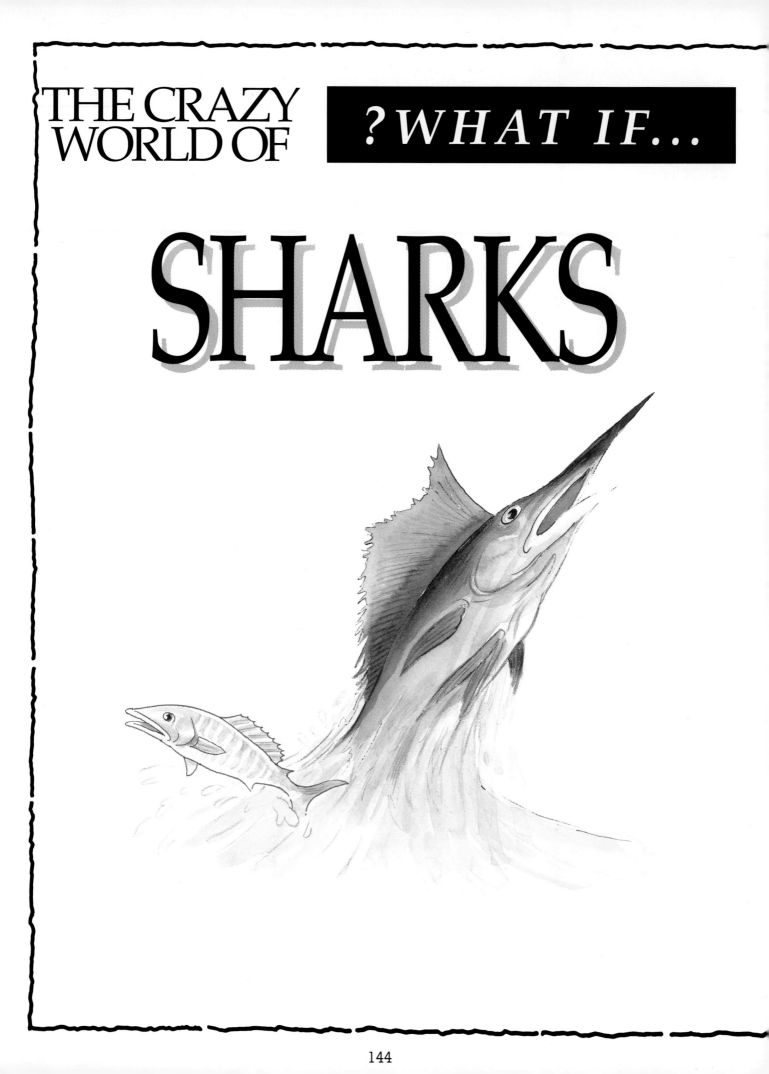

CONTENTS

146 What if sharks were the only fish?

148 What if a herring didn't have scales?

150 What if fish could fly?

152 What if fish could breathe air?

154 What if a lantern-fish couldn't see?

156 What if an angler went fishing?

158 What if salmon couldn't migrate?

160 What if sharks stopped swimming?

162 What if a seafish swam in fresh water?

164 What if coral didn't build reefs?

166 What if fish didn't swim in schools?

168 What if a plaice wasn't flat?

170 What if there were no more fish?

WHAT IF SHARKS WERE THE ONLY FISH?

Sharks form the pinnacle of an enormous food chain that exists in the world's oceans. This includes a whole host of creatures, from the smallest plankton and coral polyps to the largest fish and mammals. These incredibly diverse animals are dependent upon each other for survival. If sharks were the only fish, then there would be nothing for them to eat. They would very quickly starve and die out.

Food chain

Life in the oceans provides an endless cycle of nutrients, beginning with the tiniest, microscopic creatures. These are eaten by larger plankton, shrimp, and small fish, which in turn are eaten by larger fish, such as fry and herring. Finally, we reach the great predators, such as sharks.

When sharks die, their bodies provide food for the microscopic life. So the cycle of nutrients begins again.

What if sharks didn't have teeth?

Most sharks usually have a bristling array of very sharp teeth, set in a jaw that can be chomped together by extremely powerful muscles. These teeth are continuously replaced when they have fallen out. As the old ones fall out, new, sharper teeth that were growing behind take their place.

However, the biggest sharks, the whale shark and the basking shark, have almost no teeth at all. Instead their teeth are extremely small, and in order to eat they have to strain shrimp or plankton from the water.

Tuna

Small fry and shrimp

Plankton

Herring

Aquatic zoo

Many fish have been named after other animals because they share certain characteristics. For example, the catfish has long whiskers which it uses to feel around for food. Sea horses are unlike any other fish. They swim in an upright position with their heads bowed – like a prancing horse. The lionfish has a large mane of spines, which are tipped with a powerful poison. However, the dogfish doesn't look much like its land-living canine counterpart!

Crayfish

When is a fish not a fish?

Just as many fish have been named after other animals, so many animals have been called fish! For example, starfish belong to a group of animals called *echinoderms*, which includes sea cucumbers. Crayfish are, in fact, crustaceans, relatives of lobsters and crabs. Cuttlefish are mollusks and are similar to octopus and squid.

Some sea animals have evolved to look very similar to fish, such as whales and dolphins. These have developed the same sleek body shape as fish, but they are mammals.

Starfish

Cuttlefish

WHAT IF A HERRING DIDN'T HAVE SCALES?

A fish without scales would have much less protection against the teeth and spines of predators and enemies. It would be attacked by pests, such as fish lice and other blood-sucking parasites. It could be rubbed and cut by stones or sharp-leafed water plants. The scales of a fish act as a protective coat of armor against the outside world. Most scales are arranged like the shingles of a roof. One edge of the scale, the stalk, is attached to the skin, while the rest of the scale lies flat against the one beneath.

Some fish, like eels, have scales that are hidden by a thick, tough, slimy skin which lies on top of the scales.

Smooth customer
Fish scales are usually arranged with the stalk pointing toward the front. This lets the fish slip through the water.

Flow of water

Tough as old boots

Sharks are covered in special scales called denticles. These are tiny hooks, or teeth, that are embedded in the skin and point backward, making shark's skin extremely abrasive (rough).

They also make the skin extremely hard-wearing. So much so that jackets, vests, belts and even shoes can be made from this tough and highly durable skin.

What if a fish had no skeleton?

Fish can be split into two different groups. Those that have a skeleton made from bone, known as bony fish, and those whose skeleton is made from gristle, or cartilage, known as cartilaginous fish. Even though skeletons vary (right), they are all based on the long spinal column in the middle of the body. This is made of linked parts called vertebrae. From this ribs grow, and at the front is the skull.

The skeleton forms the fish's inner framework, upon which all of its internal organs, skin, and muscles sit. Without it, a fish would be a blob of soft tissue.

Skull

Ribs

Fin rays

Spinal column

No-bone fish
Not all fish have a skeleton made out of bone. Sharks, skates, rays, and chimaeras (e.g. ratfishes) have a skeleton made of cartilage or gristle (left). It's very strong and tough, like bone, but more flexible. These fish are called *cartilaginous fish* or chondrichthyes, and there are about 800 kinds or species.

How can you tell the age of a fish?

Most fish keep growing through life, so the biggest fish of a species are the oldest. Some types of fish, such as salmon, have scales with tiny dark lines on them. These are growth rings. Like the growth rings in a tree trunk, they tell you not only the age of a fish, but also how it has grown through its life. A group of dark lines close together shows the slow growth of one winter. A group of lines that are farther apart indicates faster growth during the summer months.

WHAT IF FISH COULD FLY?

Most fish move by swimming through the water, either by wiggling their body from side to side, or by waving their fins. A few have learned how to use their fins to walk on land (see page 153). Other fish have developed the ability to leap from the water and swoop and glide above the surface for several feet, before plunging back down into the waves. They are called flying fish.

Take off
If they are threatened by a predator, such as a shark, flying fish will gather speed, up to 20 mph (32 km/h), and shoot above the waves.

What if you could ride a sea horse?

Sea horses are true fish, cousins of pipefish and sticklebacks, but with a very strange body shape. The face resembles a horse's head, with small pectoral fins sticking from the neck, one dorsal fin on the back of the stiff body, and a curly tail to wrap around plants or rocks to hold the fish in place. Instead of getting forward movement by swishing its tail, the sea horse waves its dorsal fin very quickly to move itself forward. By swimming at a modest speed, the sea horse can suck or snap any food into its small, tube-shaped mouth.

Swooping to safety
Once the flying fish becomes airborne, it can glide for more than 330 feet (100 m) and up to 20 seconds on its outspread pectoral fins. This will take it far away from any danger.

Flapping fish
The freshwater hatchetfish of South and Central America (above) is able to fly through the air by rapidly flapping its pectoral fins, in much the same way as a bird flies.

How to swim

Although all fish swim, they don't all swim in the same way. The majority of fish, such as tuna and sharks, get the power for their forward movement from their tails, or caudal fins. Fish also need a variety of other fins around their body to control their movements. Dorsal fins keep the fish upright, while steering and braking are provided by the pectoral and the pelvic fins.

Tuna swim at more than 44 mph (70 km/h) by moving their tail from side to side. The front of the body remains fairly still.

Caudal fins

Dorsal fins

Pelvic fins

Pectoral fins

Sharks and dogfish swim by swinging their tail from side to side, while the rest of the body curves in the opposite direction.

Eels move through the water by bending their body in curves, like a snake.

WHAT IF FISH COULD BREATHE AIR?

Lungfish
The fish gulps air into gas spaces in the lung, which is a swim bladder (see page 160). Oxygen is then absorbed into blood vessels which run through it.

A few can. They are called lungfish and there are three species, found in South America, Africa, and Australia. They are able to survive underwater as well as on land, should they find themselves stranded. Other fish get all the oxygen they need to live from water. To do this they need gills, instead of the lungs that are found inside land-living animals. These feather-like organs are situated just behind the eyes, and they absorb oxygen that is dissolved in the water, into their blood.

Gas spaces

Blood vessels

Swallowed air

Gills
Fish usually have four or five sets of gills on either side of the head. They are protected by a bony plate, called *the operculum*.

Absorbing stuff
The gills are curved, red, and frilly. These frills give a large surface area as water flows over them. This allows them to absorb a great deal of oxygen very quickly. They are colored bright red because of the blood vessels that run through them. Blood flows through the gills to absorb the oxygen and carry it around the fish's body. The gills also get rid of one of the body's waste products, carbon dioxide, just as we do when we breathe out.

Water in
Water with plenty of dissolved oxygen flows in through the fish's mouth, and over the gills.

Water out
The gills take in oxygen and eliminate carbon dioxide. "Stale" water flows out of the gill slits.

A fish out of water

Several kinds of fish can survive out of water for a short time, and even move across land. They are usually fish that live in tropical swamps, such as catfish, where the pools disappear in the dry season.

The water in these pools is warm and stagnant, with little dissolved oxygen. So the catfish gulps air into pockets in the sides of the gill chambers. Oxygen goes from the air bubbles, through the watery covering of the gills, and into the blood. The gills must always be kept moist. If they dry out, the fish suffocates and dies.

Catfish

These whiskered fish, such as the upside down catfish, will travel over land, in order to get from one pond to another.

Eels

The eel wriggles through grass and plants, taking in extra oxygen through its moist, slimy, almost scaleless skin.

Mudskippers

The mudskipper lives along muddy tropical shores. It has very large gill chambers and refreshes the water in these every few minutes. It can walk on its armlike pectoral fins or surf across mud with its tail.

Bubble and squeak

Although they can't scream and shout, many fish can make noises. They do this by squeezing air bubbles that they have swallowed through their swim bladder, in just the same way as your stomach rumbles from time to time.

They can also make noises by rubbing together bones or fin spines.

The sounds may be to frighten enemies, attract mates, or keep in touch with neighbors. Some of these noisy fish are named after the sound they produce, such as drumfish, squeaker catfish, grunter gurnards, snorter horsemackerels, and singing midshipmen.

153

WHAT IF A LANTERN-FISH COULDN'T SEE?

Sight is only one of the impressive array of senses that fish use to detect the underwater world, and is only really useful in the bright, sunlit surface waters. Fish from the dim and murky midwater, between 660 and 3,300 feet (200 and 1,000 m) deep, such as the lantern fish, may have even larger eyes, to let in as much light as possible. To survive in these darker waters, as well as in the completely black depths, fish must employ their other senses to detect the world around them. Some deepsea and cavefish are totally blind and so rely entirely on their other senses. These senses include smell to scent blood in the water, touch to detect changes in currents or approaching fish, and even detection by using electrical currents.

Lens

Cornea

Retina

Lateral line

Fish eyes
Light enters the fish's eye through the transparent domed cornea. It is then bent or focused by a very thick lens, and shines onto the retina. This turns the picture into nerve signals and sends these along a nerve to the brain.

How do fish feel?

Fish can feel in the same way as humans, by detecting any direct touches on their body and fins.

They can also feel currents, swirls, and vibrations coming through the water. These are detected by the silvery stripe that runs along each side of the fish's body, called the *lateral line*. These are incredibly sensitive, and tell the fish about any underwater sounds and movements, and about the position of nearby objects. The fish can use them to sense predators or prey, and avoid bumping into rocks, even in the total darkness of the deep sea.

154

A shocking experience

Some fish use shocks of electricity to find their way, repel enemies, or stun victims (see page 157). These include the elephant-snout fish, the knifefish and torpedo-rays.

The elephant-snout fish uses electricity as a means of sensing. It makes a weak electrical field around itself by sending out pulses of electricity from its special organs. Its nose and tail detect the field, which is bent or altered by the presence of nearby creatures, rocks, and other objects. They can also detect the tiny electric charges made by another animal's muscles as it moves nearby. The elephant-snout fish grubs in the mud on the bottom and finds food such as water snails and worms, even in cloudy water.

Smelling something fishy!

Sharks use scent to detect their prey. They can "smell" certain substances in the water, even in very tiny quantities. A shark can detect the smallest drop of blood and, thinking it may be a wounded animal, may swim over looking for a meal!

Other fish use their noses to sniff out their food, as well as to recognize other fish of the same species. They are also able to tell the difference between water plants, and even the waters from different streams.

WHAT IF AN ANGLER WENT FISHING?

Fish have developed an array of different adaptations. These range from poisonous spines to inflatable bodies! They can be used either to catch something to eat, or to stop the fish from being eaten.

Anglerfish are a family of fish with a long, fleshy pole (barbel) growing from their forehead. The barbel can be colored, or even illuminated. The anglerfish goes fishing with this barbel to lure unwary prey.

Living seaweed

The leafy sea horse looks as much like a piece of seaweed as a fish. Its body is covered in leaf-like growths. When this sea horse lies still in seaweed, it is virtually impossible to spot, allowing it to hide from any predators.

Swimming plants

Many fish are masters of camouflage, hiding themselves from their prey or predators. Some have developed to look like plants. For example, pipefish (see page 159) are very thin and hang among the leaves of eelgrass, making themselves almost invisible. Those fish that cannot hide themselves have to use speed and agility to escape from being somebody's lunch.

Wobbegong

The frill around the jaw of this shark ensures that it remains hidden from its prey until the last moment. It lurks on the seabed, waiting for a scrap of food to come along.

Don't touch!

Not content with camouflage or fast swimming to avoid predators or catch prey, some fish have developed more aggressive ways to hunt or protect themselves. The electric eel and the electric catfish are able to produce intense bursts of electricity from special organs in their body, in order to stun their prey.

Others, such as the stonefish and the lionfish, have a number of poisonous spines to deter any would-be predators.

Stonefish

What if fish could blow themselves up?

There are some fish which can blow themselves up. When it is swimming about normally, the porcupinefish is covered in sharp spines to deter any would-be attackers. For extra protection, however, the fish is able to fill itself with water, inflating to become a prickly ball – not much of a tasty morsel!

Fishy cleaning staff

Cleaner wrasses are small, black-and-white striped fish which have an unusual occupation in the fish world. By performing a certain dance, the wrasse attracts other fish over to it, then proceeds to "clean" them, removing parasites from their skin and gills. The wrasse even swims into the fish's mouth without coming to harm.

Another fish, the blenny, looks very similar to the wrasse, and even attracts fish using the same dance. However, when the fish approaches, the blenny quickly darts forward and bites a chunk out of its unsuspecting visitor.

WHAT IF SALMON COULDN'T MIGRATE?

Every year, salmon swim vast distances from the sea, up the same rivers they hatched in, to reproduce. If they could not migrate, then they could not lay their eggs in the fresh water, and they would soon die out.

Fish have many bizarre ways of reproducing. Some may give birth to live young instead of laying eggs, while with others it is the male that gets pregnant!

One on one

In the vast ocean depths, you might not meet another living thing for days. Finding a mate is difficult. If a male deep-sea anglerfish meets a female, they take no chances and hang on to each other. The male grows into the body of the female and stays stuck to her. He lives off her blood and body fluids, like a parasite. When she is ready to lay her eggs, he is right there to fertilize them with his sperm.

Spawning
Exhausted after the journey, the female and male salmon spawn. She lays eggs and he sheds sperm to fertilize them.

Growing up
In spring, the eggs hatch into babies, called alevins. They grow into fry, then parr.

Little love nest

The male stickleback builds a nest from debris he has found on the river bottom. He will then try to lure a female to lay her eggs inside. The male will then deposit his sperm on the eggs to fertilize them.

The long swim home

The full-grown salmon swims back against the current of the stream in which it was born. It will probably have to negotiate many obstacles, including canal locks and waterfalls.

What if males had babies?

The males of some fish, such as sea horses and pipefish, gather eggs which have been laid by the female, and look after them while they develop. The male keeps the eggs protected in a pocketlike part on his body made of flaps of skin, called the brood pouch. When the babies hatch, they swim out of the pouch opening.

Staying at sea

Salmon may live at sea for up to five years. During this time, they grow large and sleek.

Open wide

Some cichlid fish have a peculiar way of looking after their offspring. They care for both the eggs and babies in their mouth. They are known as mouth-brooders.

When the baby cichlids have hatched, they swim in a cloud around their parent. When danger appears, the cloud of babies swims straight back into the safety of the parent's mouth.

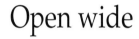

Leaving home

After four years, the parr turn silvery and become smolts. They head downriver, and out to sea.

A live birth

Most fish lay eggs, from which their young hatch. This includes sharks, whose eggs are large and in leathery cases with trailing tendrils. Empty egg cases of sharks, skates, and rays are sometimes washed up on the beach as "mermaids' purses." Other sharks, such as the white-tip shark, have eggs that hatch inside the mother, and the young emerge from the reproductive opening, called the cloaca.

WHAT IF SHARKS STOPPED SWIMMING?

They would sink to the bottom and stay there. Most fish have an inner body part like an adjustable gas bag, called a swim bladder. The fish adjusts the amount of gas in the bladder to float up or down. Sharks and other cartilaginous fish lack swim bladders and can only stay up by swimming, using their rigid fins like a plane's wings.

Some sharks need to keep swimming to get oxygen from the water into their blood. There are, however, some sharks, like some fish, that can move water over their gills without swimming, thereby getting the oxygen into their blood.

Stomach

Gills

Brain

Mouth

Heart

Liver

Which fish have wings but cannot fly?

Rays and skates are flattened cartilaginous fish. Their bodies have developed into a squashed, wing-shaped form. This is perfect for their bottom-dwelling lifestyle, where they scavenge or eat seabed creatures. While skates have a tail they can use to swim like other fish, a ray cannot swish its body from side to side, so it flaps its wings up and down to "fly" through the water.

The largest ray is the Pacific manta or devilfish. It has a "wingspan" of more than 20 feet (6 m) – about the same as a hang-glider – and weighs almost two tons. Stingrays have a sharp spine sticking out of the tail, which they can jab into enemies to inject terrible stinging poison.

Swim bladder

The fish inflates or deflates the swim bladder using gas that it has swallowed at the surface, or which is made by special organs in its body. This makes the fish more or less dense, allowing it to sink or rise in the water, like a submarine.

Swim bladder

Kidneys

Brain

Heart

Intestines

Stomach

Backbone

Kidneys

Intestines

What if a fish had no jaws?

Hagfish and lampreys (below) are two very primitive cartilaginous fish. As well as lacking bones, they do not have any movable jaws. Instead, the lamprey's mouth is a round disk armed with sharp, horny teeth. Some lampreys suck and rip chunks of flesh off bigger fish. Some even suck the blood out of a fish, like aquatic vampires!

The hagfish has a round mouth and a tongue covered in tiny teeth. It sucks and licks at the bodies of dead and dying fish, burrowing into their flesh. Once inside, it then eats the soft inner tissues.

Mistaken identity

From beneath, a surfer on a surfboard appears very similar to a seal. This may be one reason why some sharks attack humans.

Lamprey

Hagfish

161

WHAT IF A SEAFISH SWAM IN FRESH WATER?

Altogether, there are about 8,500 species of freshwater fish that swim in the many streams, rivers, and lakes throughout the world. These include the trout, the perch, and the fearsome pike.

Freshwater fish and seafish have developed bodies to cope with their own environments. There are very few fish that can live in both. If a seafish tried to swim in fresh water, it would blow up like a balloon.

Shriveled fish
A freshwater fish placed in saltwater would shrivel up. Even though it would be surrounded by water, a freshwater fish would find the sea too salty and could not control the water balance of its own body. It would rapidly lose its body fluids and die.

Giants of the rivers

The size of some freshwater fish is only governed by the availability of food and the space they are given to live in. With a lot to eat and roam in, some fish have grown to giant proportions. The arapaima of the Amazon River can reach a length of nearly 10 feet (3 m), and there are stories of it eating small children! Other river giants include the pla beuk which swims in the water of the Mekong River in China. It can grow over 10 feet (3 m), and weighs more than 530 lbs (240 kg) – that's over three times the weight of an adult human! At the other end of the scale is the Chagos dwarf goby, which is only 0.3 inches (8 mm) long.

What if fish could live in seas and rivers?

A few fish found in fresh water are able to survive in the salty sea. Salmon feed and grow in the ocean before swimming up the same river in which they were born, in order to spawn.

Common eels are actually born in the middle of the ocean. They then spend a couple of years drifting on the ocean currents, before swimming up rivers to feed and grow into adults, and then return to the sea.

Sturgeon

Salmon

Eel

Brown trout

Stealth-hunter
Pike are vicious hunters found in most northern lakes and rivers. Their slender bodies make them particularly speedy through tranquil waters. The larger pikes feed on fish, birds, and even mammals!

Hunters of rivers and lakes

As with sharks in the sea, freshwater habitats have their own hunters. In fact, there are cases in which sharks have swum into river estuaries to feed on the fish there!

Bull sharks are renowned for this, and have even attacked people who thought they were safe in the freshwater estuaries of rivers.

Other fishy hunters, like piranha, swarm together in large, powerful schools, looking for something to eat. If they come across a fish or other animal that shows signs of being wounded or in trouble, these fish will attack, and eat the creatures in a matter of seconds.

WHAT IF CORAL DIDN'T BUILD REEFS?

We wouldn't have some of the richest and most colorful wildlife habitats on the planet, and the many fish that populate the reefs would be left without a home. Reefs are massive natural structures that are built by tiny animals, called coral polyps. The Great Barrier Reef, off the coast of Australia, stretches over 1,250 miles (2,000 km).

The reef forms only one of many coastal environments, which can also include mudflats, sandbanks, rocky shores, and beaches. The shallow waters are packed full of food, such as seaweeds and invertebrate (backbone-less) animals that a huge diversity of fish, from clownfish to sharks, can feed on.

Biodiversity
A patch of seashore in North America or Europe might have 50 different fish species. A same-sized patch of tropical coral reef could have 500, as well as other animals, from anemones to starfish.

What if a fish had a beak?

The parrotfish found swimming around many coral reefs is so called because it has a hard, horny mouth, rather like the beak of a parrot. This has been formed by the fish's teeth that have fused together.

The parrotfish uses its hard mouth to scrape at the stony skeletons that the coral have left behind. It does not feed on the rock itself, but on the tiny coral animals and other small creatures. As the fish clears a patch and moves on, new coral polyps and other creatures settle on the exposed rock. The whole process usually balances out, so while the fish is feeding itself, the coral polyps continue to build the reef.

Shedding light

Coastal waters have such an incredible wealth of creatures because of the sunlight that can reach the seabed. Here, plants and coral convert this large amount of sunlight into energy, to grow. With this rich basis of plants and simple animals, such as plankton, coastal waters teem with fish and other animals.

Hiding places

The many nooks and crannies scattered throughout the coral reef offer excellent hiding places for both hunters and hunted.

Fishy sleeping bag

During the night, day-active (diurnal) fish settle and rest in the reef. One type of parrotfish even makes a covering of mucus around itself, like a slimy sleeping bag. This traps a layer of water around this fish, and protects it should the fish be attacked, or exposed by the retreating tide. Meanwhile, as darkness falls, night-active (nocturnal) fish and other animals, such as sea urchins and starfish, come out to feed.

Predators

Sharks, barracuda, and other large fish cruise the reef, looking for a victim that is old, injured, sick, or off guard.

Disappearing grass

Garden eels and sand eels live in tube-shaped burrows on the seabed. As they poke out the front part of the body to catch food floating past, they look like a patch of waving grass. Should danger loom, the eels quickly whisk down into their burrows. In less than a second, the lawn of eels has disappeared into the sandy sea floor.

WHAT IF FISH DIDN'T SWIM IN SCHOOLS?

They might easily be caught and eaten by one of the ocean's many hunters! Some species of fish, particularly those found in the open ocean, such as cod and herring, form themselves into enormous groups called *shoals*, or schools. These schools can have as few as 25 individuals, or as many as several thousand fish, all of them swimming in the same direction. These schools have nothing to do with education. Instead, the dense collections of fish protect themselves by dazzling the hunter with a silvery blur. Other open-water fish have developed weapons or incredible speed to avoid predators or catch their prey.

Open ocean sword-fighter

The swordfish has a long, sharp, pointed nose, much like a sword. It uses this to defend itself, and also to stun and kill its prey with slashing strokes. The sharp nose also helps to make the fish extremely streamlined, allowing it to slice through the water at very high speeds.

Underwater pilots

The pilotfish swims very near other large sea animals, such as sharks, giving the impression that it is guiding the bigger creature. This is not the case. Instead, this small, striped fish merely follows the creature around the water. It can feed on any scraps of food that the shark leaves after it has made a kill. Pilotfish are extremely agile and so can easily dodge a lumbering shark if it tries to eat them.

What is the fastest fish?

The fastest fish in the world live in the oceans, far from shore. They need their speed either to dodge predators or catch prey. Over short distances the sailfish is the quickest thing in the water. In short bursts, it can swim at an amazing speed of nearly 70 mph (110 km/h). To achieve this, its body needs to be extremely streamlined, otherwise the turbulence it creates in the water would slow it down. The streamlining is further enhanced by its almost scaleless skin. In parts of the body where there are scales, they are set well below the skin's surface to prevent them causing turbulence. Other very fast fish include the wahoo and the blue-fin tuna. These can swim at more than 40 mph (65 km/h).

Sailfish

Wahoo

WHAT IF A PLAICE WASN'T FLAT?

Ten-day-old plaice

Two-week-old plaice

Then it wouldn't be able to lie on the seabed without other fish noticing it. Many bottom-dwelling fish have developed a flat body and camouflage pattern in order to blend in with the sea floor. Whereas rays and skates are flattened from top to bottom, flatfish like plaice are flattened on their sides. As they develop from a normal-looking young fish, one of the eyes "migrates" to the other side of the body. The body gradually becomes thinner, and before long the fish is lying and swimming on its side!

Three-week-old plaice

Migrating eye

What if gulper eels had small mouths?

The gulper eel is one of many bizarre-looking fish that inhabit the murky depths of the world's oceans. Basically, it is an enormous swimming mouth! This mouth is capable of opening and expanding to huge proportions, allowing the eel to swallow fish many times its own size. Once the fish has been swallowed whole, it is slowly digested within the eel's stomach. Not surprisingly, the eel does not have to eat again for a long time. Without its huge gape, the eel would have to pick on smaller fry for its supper.

Adult plaice

Fish on stilts

The tripod fish gets its name from the three highly developed fins that hang beneath its body. When the tripod fish isn't swimming through the dark deep ocean, it rests on the seabed. It uses its elongated fins like a set of stilts, keeping its body above the slimy ooze and mud that coat the sea floor.

Once on the seabed, the tripod fish can "walk" along the bottom, as it waits for any morsels of food to come along. Other fish that rest and "walk" on their fins are lizardfish and some types of gurnards.

Now you see me, now you don't!
Some bottom-dwelling flatfish, such as plaice, can vary the color of their skin, just like a chameleon! They can blend in with the sea floor, and lie undisturbed by predators.

What if fish had flashlights?

Nearly 80% of all fish found in the darkness of the deep sea are able to produce light from special organs on their bodies. Some, such as deep-sea anglerfish and viperfish, use a light on the end of a pole to lure prey (see page 156). Others, such as lantern fish and hatchetfish, use downward pointing light organs in order to blend in with any sunlight that filters down from above. This will keep them camouflaged from predators that may be swimming below. Some fish use their lights in order to frighten off other fish that may eat them for lunch.

Hatchetfish

Viperfish

Lantern fish

WHAT IF THERE WERE NO MORE FISH?

In some lakes and rivers, and in some parts of the oceans, there are hardly any fish left. They have all been caught in nets or on lines, as food for people, pets, and farm animals; or they have been hooked by anglers for sport; or the water is so dirty and polluted that fish and other creatures cannot survive.

Many animals and plants rely on fish, whether it is the meat of their bodies or the nutrients from their decaying corpses. Either way, fish form a vital part of the watery ecosystem. If they were to disappear, as may happen in some parts of the world, the effects on the environment could be disastrous – many other species of animal could die out, too.

Global trash bin

Every day we humans dump thousands of tons of garbage, waste, and chemicals into the streams, rivers, and oceans of the world. But we hardly ever see the damage this causes. We might notice an otter or a seabird on the surface, covered with oil from a ship that has illegally washed out its tanks. But we don't notice the thousands of fish suffocating and dying below the surface. The animal and plant life in many rivers and parts of the seas has been killed off by heavy pollution.

Birds
Dozens of seabird species, including albatrosses, cormorants, terns, pelicans, penguins, and many other birds, eat lots of fish. Without this source of food, they would starve.

Mammals

The many mammals that rely on fish to eat would probably become extinct. These include seals, dolphins, hunting whales, and otters.

Invertebrates

Squid, octopuses, crabs, lobsters, jellyfish, anemones, and many other invertebrates (animals without backbones) hunt or catch a huge variety of fish to eat; or they might feed off their decaying bodies. Without fish, they may turn on each other for food.

What if fish were grown on farms?

Fish farming is carried out in many parts of the world. Trout, catfish, carp, and similar fish are grown in huge tanks or sealed lakes. They are fed and given clean, fresh water. Salmon and other saltwater fish are grown in huge wire-mesh cages suspended in the sea. They are also protected in these farms.

As a result, we have been able to provide a reliable source of fish. Before long we may be able to use fish farming to get all of our fish, without having to deplete natural fish stocks in the sea.

Disappearing fish stocks

Modern fishing is big business, with modern fishing boats, using sonar equipment to find schools of fish, and enormous nets to catch them in. Every day these fleets of trawlers take vast quantities of fish from the sea.

However, the size of the fish and the number of fish taken has been decreasing in many parts of the oceans. In some places, such as the Grand Banks off the coast of Canada, fish have virtually disappeared. The fish cannot breed quickly enough to replace the numbers that humans catch.

GLOSSARY

Airfoil section
The special shape of an aircraft wing or propeller when seen edge-on, with the upper surface more curved than the lower surface. This gives a difference in air pressure and creates the force called *lift.*

Asteroid
A small, rocky body also known as a minor planet. In our solar system the greatest concentration of asteroids is in the asteroid belt between the planets Mars and Jupiter.

Atmosphere
Air, the mixture of gases around the Earth, which gradually thins out above heights of 60-120 miles into space. It has four main layers – the troposphere, stratosphere, mesosphere, and thermosphere.

Atoll
These are caused by corals growing on the sides of an oceanic volcano. The volcano, worn away by weather, slowly submerges and a ring of low-lying coral islands, or atolls, are left.

Biodiversity
The number of different species of plants or animals found in one area.

Black hole
A region in space that has a gravity so strong that nothing can escape from it.

Blubber
A thick layer of fat found in some sea mammals which helps to keep them warm in the cold sea.

Bony fish
A fish whose skeleton is made from bone.

Cartilaginous fish
A fish whose skeleton is made from cartilage.

Control surface
A panel on an aircraft that moves into the air flowing past, and helps to control the flight path.

Core
The innermost, middle, or central part of an object, such as the Earth. This is divided into the outer core – about 1,400 miles thick, and slightly flexible or "plastic," and an inner core – 1,700 miles across and solid.

Crust
The thin, hard outer layer which surrounds the Earth. Under the continents, the crust is 12-25 miles thick. Under the oceans it is much thinner, 3-7 miles thick.

Digestion
The breakdown and absorption of food into your body.

Diurnal
An animal that is awake during the day and sleeps at night.

Enzymes
Chemicals that increase the rate of a chemical change or reaction. In the case of digestion they break down large food particles to help the body absorb them.

Evolution
The changes that all living things have undergone in order to adapt to their environment over time.

Fin
Airplanes – the "tail," the upright part or vertical stabilizer, which is usually at the rear of an airplane.
Sharks – the parts of the body that fish use to control their movement.

Fur
A coat of hair that covers many mammals and keeps them warm (and cool!).

Fuselage
The main "body" of a plane, which is usually a long, thin tube carrying the crew, passengers, and freight.

Galaxy
A huge group or cluster of stars separated from other galaxies by vast empty space. Our own galaxy is called the Galaxy or Milky Way.

Gills
The featherlike organs in some animals that absorb oxygen from the water as it flows over them.

Gravity
Gravitational force is the natural attracting force or pull exerted by all objects on all other objects. It is one of the four basic forces in the universe. The Sun's gravity keeps the Earth moving around it. The Earth's gravity pulls us and all other

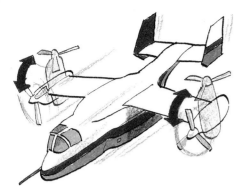

objects down toward its center.

Hearing
The sense that allows you to pick up sounds using your ears.

Heart
The organ that pushes blood around the blood vessels.

Herd
A group of animals, ranging from a small family group to millions of different creatures.

Hibernation
The deep "sleep" that some creatures undergo during the winter months.

Lateral line
The line that runs down the length of the fish on either side. It is extremely sensitive and detects any vibrations in the water.

Lithosphere
The rigid outer shell of the Earth, about 60 miles deep. It includes the crust and the outer part of the mantle. It is divided jigsawlike into large lithospheric plates, whose slow movements cause continental drift.

Lungs
A pair of organs that are the sites of oxygen absorption.

Mach
A speed scale related to the speed of sound. Mach 1 is the speed of sound under given conditions such as pressure and temperature. This term is named after the Austrian scientist, Ernst Mach (1838-1916)

Magnetism

A force that can attract or repel objects containing iron. Electromagnetic force is one of the four basic forces in the universe.

Mantle
The thickest layer of the Earth under the outer crust, about 1,800 miles deep. Its rocks are hot and flow very slowly, creating the Earth's natural magnetic field.

Marsupial
Animals who give birth to very undeveloped young who then develop and grow inside the mother's pouch.

Meteor
Material from space that enters the Earth's atmosphere, glows with friction as it rushes through the air, and then burns up – a "shooting star." A meteorite is a meteor which has fallen to the Earth's surface.

Monotreme
A mammal that lays eggs instead of giving birth to live young.

Nocturnal
A creature that is asleep during the day and awake at night.

Orbit
The curved path of an object as it goes around a larger one. The Moon orbits the Earth, and the Earth orbits the Sun. Most orbits are oval shaped, called an *ellipse*.

Ozone Layer

A layer of atmosphere containing a form of normal oxygen gas – ozone. The ozone is mostly 10-28 miles above the earth, and is very thinly spread out compared to the other atmosphere gases. It helps to absorb harmful ultraviolet (UV) rays from the Sun, thereby protecting all living things.

Pitch
The angle of a plane when seen from the side – that is whether it is

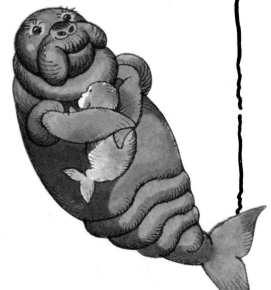

pointing up – climbing, or down – diving.

Planet
A relatively large object that goes around a star, such as the nine planets orbiting the Sun.

Predator
An animal that actively hunts, kills, and eats other creatures.

Primate
The group of animals including monkeys, apes, and humans.

Pulse
The rate at which your heart beats.

Quasar
(Quasi-stellar object) A mysterious and extremely distant object that shines like many galaxies, but which

GLOSSARY

seems smaller in size than one galaxy. It may be a galaxy being born.

Red blood cells
The doughnut-shaped cell that gives blood its red color.

Respiration
The overall exchange of oxygen and carbon dioxide between lungs, blood, body cells, and the atmosphere.

Rotors
The long propeller-like blades on top of a helicopter, which provide lift and also allow the helicopter to fly

forward, backward, and sideways.

Ruminant
A plant-eating mammal with a four-chambered stomach, that is capable of regurgitating its food to chew again and so aid digestion.

Satellite
An object in space that orbits a larger object. So Earth is a satellite of the Sun, and the Moon is a satellite of the Earth. But the word "satellite" is usually used to mean an artificial or man-made space object.

Shoal
A group of fish that swim together. They can number up to several thousand. Also called a school.

Sight
The sense that lets you see the world around you using your eyes.

Skeleton
The structure that supports the body of a living organism.

Smell
The sense that allows you to experience odors, using smell cells in the roof of the nasal cavity.

Solar system
A group of planets that orbit a star. Our solar system has a total of nine planets that move around the Sun.

Spawn
When fish reproduce, it is called spawning.

Spiracle
An opening on an insect's skin that lets air into its breathing system.

Star
In astronomy, a star is an object that gives out energy as light, heat, and other forms of radiation.

STOL
Short Take-Off and Landing, meaning an aircraft that can go up or come down on a short runway. This can be a couple of hundred feet long.

Swim bladder
The spongy organ inside all bony fish which helps them to regulate the depth at which they swim.

Taste
The sense that lets you experience flavors, using taste buds on the tongue and upper throat.

Touch
The sense that allows you to feel the world around you. The majority of touch sensors are found in the skin.

Turbine
Set of fanlike angled blades used in machines such as power plant generators and aircraft engines.

Universe
All galaxies, stars, planets, as well as the space, cosmic dust, and all other matter between them.

Variable geometry
The proper name for a "swing-wing" plane, where the main wings usually swing straight out sideways for slow flight or takeoff, and sweep backward for fast flight.

Valve
A flaplike part of the blood system found in the heart and some veins. These close to stop blood from flowing the wrong way around the blood system.

White blood cell
These cells protect the body from foreign invaders, such as bacteria.

White dwarf
A small type or stage in the life of a star, possibly not much bigger than planets such as Jupiter. It is usually a star that is reaching the end of its life.

Yaw
The angle of a plane when seen from above or below – that is, whether it is flying straight ahead, or turning

meteor 10, 32, 173
meteorite 10, 14, 173
Microlight 50
MiG 52
migration 65, 67, 158, 159
milk 126, 128, 129, 131
Mir 31
mollusc 143
monotreme 126, 173
Moon 8, 14-15, 24, 29, 64, 67, 70, 71
mountains 73, 79
mouth 100–101
muscles 38, 39, 91, 92-93, 98, 116

NASA 25
navigation 56
nebulae 10, 18, 19
nerves 90, 93, 100, 106-107, 116
nocturnal 133, 165, 173
North Pole 64, 66, 68, 86
nose 100–101
nuclear fusion 19, 21

oceans 77, 78
orbit 65, 69, 76, 173
Orion's belt 20
ovaries 113
oxygen 96, 97
ozone layer 86, 173

pancreas 103, 116
Phillips Multiplane 41
pilot 39, 42, 45, 45, 47, 50, 51, 54-57, 59
  autopilot 54
plankton 146, 147, 165
plant-eater 131, 134
plants 68, 78, 82
planet 8, 10, 12, 13, 14, 16, 22, 173
  Jupiter 8, 10, 13, 15, 16, 69

Mars 10, 13, 31, 32, 69
Mercury 10, 13, 69
Neptune 13
Pluto 13
Saturn 12, 13, 15, 17
Venus 10, 12, 32, 69
poison 147, 156, 157, 160
pollen 77
pollution 76, 86, 87, 170
pouch 126, 127, 129
predator 129, 131, 134, 146, 173
pregnancy 113
primate 139, 173
propeller 36, 46-47, 50-51, 53

radar 37, 41, 54, 56
radio 56, 57, 59, 67
radio telescopes 9, 22
radio wave 10, 30
rain 78, 79, 81, 82
rainforests 78, 87
red giant 18
reproduction 112, 113, 158-159
reptiles 126, 127
retina 109
rivers 78
rocket 11, 26-27, 37, 45, 55
  boosters 27
  multi-staged 27
rotor 46, 47, 174
ruminant 135, 174

saltwater fish 162-163, 171
satellite 9, 10, 11, 23, 25, 26, 27, 29, 37, 56, 57, 174
scales 148-149, 167
  denticles 148
  stalks 148
scent 125, 133, 134
schools 166, 174
seaplane 42-43, 55
sea urchins 165

seasons 65, 69, 76
sedimentary rocks 73
sharks 146, 149, 150, 151, 155, 159, 160, 163, 164, 165, 167
  attacks 161
  basking 146
  whale 146
  white-tip 159
  wobbegong 156
sight 125, 133, 154, 174
skeleton 94–95, 116, 149, 174
skin 90–91, 114
  dermis 90, 91
  epidermis 90
smell 101, 154, 155, 174
soil 82–83
solar system 8, 12-13, 30, 174
sonar 124
sound 19, 124, 133, 153, 154
South Pole 64, 66, 68, 86
spacecraft 24-25
  Apollo II 14, 24
  Luna 3 15
  Sputnik I 11, 24
  Vostok I 24
space probe 12-13, 17, 32, 33
Space Race 24
space shuttle 27, 37, 49
spacesuit 11, 24, 28-29
sperm 113
spine 147, 148, 156, 157, 160
spleen 103
star 8, 9, 10, 18, 19, 20-21, 22, 32, 174
  charts 20, 21
  shooting star 10
  star map 33
stealth plane 41
STOL 53, 58, 174

stomach 92, 102–103, 117
storms 80-81
Sun 8, 9, 10, 13, 15, 16, 17, 18, 21, 64, 65, 67, 69, 76, 78, 79, 84, 85, 86, 87
supercluster 23
supernova 18
swim bladders 152, 160-161, 174

tail 40-41
taste 100, 101, 174
teeth 100, 134, 136-137, 146, 161, 164
telescope 8-9, 15, 17, 23, 33
thermals 39, 48, 49
tidal wave 81
tongue 101, 106
tornadoes 80
touch 154, 174
trees 68, 76, 78, 83, 85, 87

UFO 32
ultraviolet rays 86
universe 9, 16, 22-23, 30, 31, 174

volcanoes 73, 74-75

water 78–79, 81, 85
weather 76–77, 78, 79, 80-81, 87
weather balloons 27
whale 97, 99, 114, 121, 124, 143, 147, 171
white dwarf 18, 174
wind 76-77, 80, 81, 85
wings 36-37, 38, 39, 41, 43, 47, 50, 60, 133, 160
Wright brothers 44, 45

X rays 9, 10, 19, 30

Yaw 174

INDEX

aircraft carrier 43, 59
airfoil 37, 50, 60, 172
airport 42, 58-59
air-traffic controller 56, 57, 59
alien 15, 32, 33
Armstrong, Neil 24,
arteries 98
asteroid belt 10, 14, 69, 172
astronomer 13
astronaut 14, 24, 26, 28, 29, 31
atmosphere 11, 12, 13, 24, 172

Beaufort Scale 76
bird 11, 36, 38, 39
Blackbird 37, 45
"black box" 55
black hole 19, 172
Blériot, Louis 44
blood 98, 99, 117
  clots 99
  circulation 117
  red blood cells 95, 99, 174
  white blood cells 95, 99, 105, 174
blubber 123, 128, 172
bones 94–95, 116
  ankle 94, 116
  backbone 94, 116
  cervical vertebrae 116
  ribs 96, 116
  wrist 94
brain 106–107, 117
breathing 96–97, 116
brood pouches 159
bruises 90

camouflage 122-123, 156, 157, 168, 169
carnivore 137
cartilaginous fish 149, 160, 161, 172
cerebral cortex 107
Channel Tunnel 61
claw 133, 136
cockpit 48

comet 8, 16, 17
  Halley's 17
commuter planes 58
compass 66-67
Concorde 41
conservation 141
continents 72-73
controls 46, 47, 54
coral reefs 74, 164-165
  atoll 74
crustaceans 147

DarkStar 37
deserts 77
diaphragm 96
digestion 117, 172
diurnal 133, 172

ears 110–111
earthquakes 75
Earth's crust 72, 74, 172
eclipse 9, 15
elbow 93
electricity 81, 84, 85, 154, 155, 157
energy 69
  geothermal 84
  light 87
  nuclear 84
  solar 84, 85
  tidal 85
  water 85
  wind 85
engine 11, 36, 37, 41, 44, 47, 48-49, 50, 51, 52, 53
  jet 36, 51, 52-53,
  rotary engine 53
enzymes 172
equator 68, 76
Everest 73
eyes 108-109, 116

feeding 128, 129, 134-135
fighter plane 41, 43, 51, 52
fin 40, 41, 150, 151, 153, 154, 160, 169, 172

fish farming 171
flight deck 57
flood 81, 87
"Flying Bedstead" 36
flying fish 150, 151
fossil fuel 84-85
freshwater fish 151, 162-163
fuel 56
fur 122, 123, 127, 172
fuselage 42, 60, 172

Gagarin, Yuri 24
galaxy 9, 20, 22, 23, 31, 32, 172
  Andromeda 23, 31
  elliptical 20
  irregular 20
  local group 23, 31
  Milky Way 9, 20
  spiral 20, 21
Galileo Galilei 8
gamma rays 9
gases 12, 16, 17, 18, 29
germs 99, 100, 105
gestation 126
geysers 75, 84
gills 96, 152-153, 157, 160, 172
glider 36, 38, 39, 44, 48, 49, 55
  hang glider 48
  military glider 49
Global Positioning Satellite 67
global warming 86
Gossamer Albatross 39
gravity 26, 31, 68, 70, 71, 172
Great Red Spot 13
greenhouse effect 87
gullet 102

Halley, Edmond 17
Harrier jump jet 36, 43
hearing 110-111, 173
heart 96, 98–99, 104, 173

helicopter 43, 46-47
herbivore see plant-eater
herd 130, 131, 134, 135, 173
hibernation 65, 132, 173
hovercraft 36, 43
hurricanes 81
hydrofoil 43

ice 13
igneous rocks 73
insects 87, 95, 97, 100
intestines 103, 117
invertebrates 164, 171

jets 36, 43, 45, 52-53, 55, 57, 58, 59, 61
  combat jets 41, 43
  ramjet 52
  turbofan 51, 52, 53

kidneys 103, 117

lava 73, 74
Leonov, Alexei 29
lift 36, 37, 38, 43, 46, 47, 60
lightning 81
light-year 23, 30
Lindbergh, Charles 45
liver 102, 117
lungs 96, 99, 117, 173
lymph 105

Mach 41, 173
magma 72, 74
magnetism 66-67, 173
mammary gland 128
mantle 74, 173
marrow 95
marsupial 126, 127, 173
mermaids' purses 159
metabolism 132
metamorphic rocks 73